ARCHIVE FEVER

RELIGION AND POSTMODERNISM
A Series Edited by Mark C. Taylor

Archive
Fever

A FREUDIAN IMPRESSION

JACQUES DERRIDA

TRANSLATED BY ERIC PRENOWITZ

THE UNIVERSITY OF CHICAGO PRESS *Chicago & London*

The University of Chicago Press, Chicago 60637
The University of Chicago Press, Ltd., London
© 1995 The Johns Hopkins University Press
Translator's Note © 1996 by The University of Chicago
All rights reserved.
University of Chicago Press edition published 1996
Paperback edition 1998
Printed in the United States of America
05 04 03 02 01 00 99 98   2 3 4 5

ISBN: 0-226-14336-8 (cloth)
ISBN: 0-226-14367-8 (paperback)

Originally published as *Mal d'Archive: une impression freudienne,*
© Éditions Galilée, 1995. Translation first published in *Diacritics,* Summer 1995.

Library of Congress Cataloging-in-Publication Data

Derrida, Jacques.
      [Mal d'archive. English]
      Archive fever : a Freudian impression / Jacques Derrida ;
   translated by Eric Prenowitz.
            p.   cm. — (Religion and postmodernism)
      Originally presented as a lecture June 5, 1994, at a colloquium in London,
   England.
      Includes bibliographical references (p.   ).
      ISBN 0-226-14336-8 (cloth)
      1. Memory (Philosophy)   2. Psychoanalysis.   3. Freud, Sigmund, 1856–
   1939.   I. Title.   II. Series.
   BD181.7.D4713   1996
   153.1'2—dc20   96-18568
                                                                         CIP

Contents

Lecture given on 5 June 1994 in London during an international colloquium entitled "Memory: The Question of Archives." Organized at the initiative of René Major and Elisabeth Roudinesco, the colloquium was held under the auspices of the Société Internationale d'Histoire de la Psychiatrie et de la Psychanalyse, of the Freud Museum, and of the Courtauld Institute of Art.

The original title of this lecture, "The Concept of the Archive: A Freudian Impression," was modified afterward. (The French title is *Mal d'Archive: une impression freudienne*.)

Let us not begin at the beginning, nor even at the archive.

But rather at the word "archive"—and with the archive of so familiar a word. *Arkhē,* we recall, names at once the *commencement* and the *commandment.* This name apparently coordinates two principles in one: the principle according to nature or history, *there* where things *commence*—physical, historical, or ontological principle—but also the principle according to the law, *there* where men and gods *command, there* where authority, social order are exercised, *in this place* from which *order* is given—nomological principle.

There, we said, and *in this place.* How are we to think of *there?* And this *taking place* or this *having a place* of the *arkhē?*

We have *there* two orders of order: *sequential* and *jussive.* From this point on, a series of cleavages will incessantly divide every atom of our lexicon. Already in the *arkhē* of the commencement, I alluded to the commencement according to nature *or* according to history, introducing surreptitiously a chain of belated and problematic oppositions between *physis* and its others, *thesis, tekhnē, nomos,* etc., which are found to be at work in the other principle, the nomological principle of the *arkhē,* the principle of the commandment. All would be simple if there were one principle or two principles. All would be simple if the *physis* and each one of its others were one or two. As we have suspected for a long time, it is nothing of the sort, yet we are forever forgetting this. There is always more than one—and more or less than two. In the order of the commencement as well as in the order of the commandment.

The concept of the archive shelters in itself, of course, this memory of the name *arkhē*. But it also *shelters* itself from this memory which it shelters: which comes down to saying also that it forgets it. There is nothing accidental or surprising about this. Contrary to the impression one often has, such a concept is not easy to archive. One has trouble, and for essential reasons, establishing it and interpreting it in the document it delivers to us, here in the word which names it, that is the "archive." In a way, the term indeed refers, as one would correctly believe, to the *arkhē* in the *physical, historical,* or *ontological* sense, which is to say to the originary, the first, the principial, the primitive, in short to the commencement. But even more, and *even earlier,* "archive" refers to the *arkhē* in the *nomological* sense, to the *arkhē* of the commandment. As is the case for the Latin *archivum* or *archium* (a word that is used in the singular, as was the French *archive,* formerly employed as a masculine singular: *un archive*), the meaning of "archive," its only meaning, comes to it from the Greek *arkheion*: initially a house, a domicile, an address, the residence of the superior magistrates, the *archons,* those who commanded. The citizens who thus held and signified political power were considered to possess the right to make or to represent the law. On account of their publicly recognized authority, it is at their home, in that *place* which is their house (private house, family house, or employee's house), that official documents are filed. The archons are first of all the documents' guardians. They do not only ensure the physical security of what is deposited and of the substrate. They are also accorded the hermeneutic right and competence. They have the power to interpret the archives. Entrusted to such archons, these documents in effect speak the law: they recall the law and call on or impose the law. To be guarded thus, in the jurisdiction of this *speaking the law,* they needed at once a guardian and a localization. Even in their guardianship or their hermeneutic tradition, the archives could do neither without substrate nor without residence.

It is thus, in this *domiciliation,* in this house arrest, that archives take place. The dwelling, this place where they dwell permanently, marks this institutional passage from the private to the public, which does not always mean from the secret to the nonsecret. (It is what is happening, right here, when a house, the Freuds' last house, becomes a museum: the passage from one institution to another.) With such a status, the documents, which are not always discursive writings, are only kept and classified under the title of the archive by virtue of a privileged *topology*. They inhabit this uncommon place, this place of election where law and singularity intersect in *privilege*. At the intersection of the topological and the nomological, of the place and the law, of the substrate and the authority, a scene of domiciliation becomes at once visible and invisible. I stress this point for reasons which will, I hope, appear more clearly later. They all have to do with this *topo-nomology*, with this archontic dimension of domiciliation, with this archic, in truth patriarchic, function, without which no archive would ever come into play or appear as such. To shelter itself and, sheltered, to conceal itself. This archontic function is not solely topo-nomological. It does not only require that the archive be deposited somewhere, on a stable substrate, and at the disposition of a legitimate hermeneutic authority. The archontic power, which also gathers the functions of unification, of identification, of classification, must be paired with what we will call the power of *consignation*. By consignation, we do not only mean, in the ordinary sense of the word, the act of assigning residence or of entrusting so as to put into reserve (to consign, to deposit), in a place and on a substrate, but here the act of *con*signing through *gathering together signs*. It is not only the traditional *consignatio*, that is, the written proof, but what all *consignatio* begins by presupposing. *Consignation* aims to coordinate a single corpus, in a system or a synchrony in which all the elements articulate the unity of an ideal configuration. In an archive, there should not be any absolute dissociation, any heterogeneity or *secret* which could separate (*secernere*), or partition, in an absolute manner. The archontic principle of the archive is also a principle of consignation, that is, of gathering together.

It goes without saying from now on that wherever one could attempt, and in particular in Freudian psychoanalysis, to rethink the place and the law according to which the archontic becomes instituted, wherever one could interrogate or contest, directly or indirectly, this archontic principle, its authority, its titles, and its genealogy, the right that it commands, the legality or the legitimacy that depends on it, wherever secrets and heterogeneity would seem to menace even the possibility of *consignation,* this can only have grave consequences for a theory of the archive, as well as for its institutional implementation. A science of the archive must include the theory of this institutionalization, that is to say, the theory both of the law which begins by inscribing itself there and of the right which authorizes it. This right imposes or supposes a bundle of limits which have a history, a deconstructable history, and to the deconstruction of which psychoanalysis has not been foreign, to say the least. This deconstruction in progress concerns, as always, the institution of limits *declared* to be insurmountable,[1] whether they involve family or state law, the relations between the secret and the nonsecret, or, and this is not the same thing, between the private and the public, whether they involve property or access rights, publication or reproduction rights, whether they involve classification and putting *into order:* What comes under theory or under private

1. Of course, the question of a politics of the archive is our permanent orientation here, even if the time of a lecture does not permit us to treat this directly and with examples. This question will never be determined as one political question among others. It runs through the whole of the field and in truth determines politics from top to bottom as *res publica.* There is no political power without control of the archive, if not of memory. Effective democratization can always be measured by this essential criterion: the participation in and the access to the archive, its constitution, and its interpretation. *A contrario,* the breaches of democracy can be measured by what a recent and in so many ways remarkable work entitles *Forbidden Archives (Archives interdites: Les peurs françaises face à l'histoire contemporaine).* Under this title, which we cite as the metonymy of all that is important here, Sonia Combe does not only gather a considerable collection of material, to illuminate and interpret it; she asks numerous essential questions about the writing of history, about the "repression" of the archive [318], about the "'repressed' archive" as "power . . . of the state over the historian" [321]. Among all of these questions, and in referring the reader to this book, let us isolate here the one that is consonant, in a way, with the low tone of our hypothesis, even if this fundamental note, the patriarchive, never covers all the others. As if in passing, Sonia Combe asks in effect: "I hope to be pardoned for granting some credit to the following observation, but it does not seem to me to be due to pure chance that the corporation of well-known historians of contemporary France is essentially, apart from a few exceptions, masculine. . . . But I hope to be understood also . . ." [315].

4

correspondence, for example? What comes under system? under biography or autobiography? under personal or intellectual anamnesis? In works said to be *theoretical,* what is worthy of this name and what is not? Should one rely on what Freud says about this to classify his works? Should one for example take him at his word when he presents his *Moses* as a "historical novel"? In each of these cases, the limits, the borders, and the distinctions have been shaken by an earthquake from which no classificational concept and no implementation of the archive can be sheltered. Order is no longer assured.

I dream now of having the time to submit for your discussion more than one thesis, three at least. This time will never be given to me. Above all, I will never have the right to take your time so as to impose upon you, rapid-fire, these three + *n* essays. Submitted to the test of your discussion, these theses thus remain, for the time being, hypotheses. Incapable of supporting their demonstration, constrained to posit them along the way in a mode which will appear at times dogmatic, I will recall them in a more critical and formal manner in conclusion.

The hypotheses have a common trait. They all concern the *impression* left, in my opinion, by the *Freudian signature* on its own archive, on the concept of the archive and of archivization, that is to say also, inversely and as an indirect consequence, on historiography. Not only on historiography in general, not only on the history of the concept of the archive, but perhaps also on the history of the formation of a *concept in general.* We are saying for the time being *Freudian signature* so as not to have to decide yet between Sigmund Freud, the proper name, on the one hand, and, on the other, the invention of psychoanalysis: project of knowledge, of practice and of institution, community, family, domiciliation, consignation, "house" or "museum," in the present state of its archivization. What is in question is situated precisely *between the two.*

Having thus announced my intentions, and promised to collect them so as to conclude in a more organized fashion, I ask your permission to take the time and the liberty to enter upon several lengthy preliminary excursions.

Exergue

According to a proven convention, the *exergue* plays with citation. To cite before beginning is to give the tone through the resonance of a few words, the meaning or form of which ought to set the stage. In other words, the exergue consists in capitalizing on an ellipsis. In accumulating capital in advance and in preparing the surplus value of an archive. An exergue serves to stock in anticipation and to prearchive a lexicon which, from there on, ought to lay down the law and *give the order,* even if this means contenting itself with naming the problem, that is, the subject. In this way, the exergue has at once an institutive and a conservative function: the violence of a power (*Gewalt*) which at once posits and conserves the law, as the Benjamin of *Zur Kritik der Gewalt* would say. What is at issue here, starting with the exergue, is the violence of the archive itself, *as archive, as archival violence.*

It is thus the first figure of an archive, because *every* archive, we will draw some inferences from this, is at once *institutive* and *conservative.* Revolutionary and traditional. An *eco-nomic* archive in this double sense: it keeps, it puts in reserve, it saves, but in an unnatural fashion, that is to say in making the law (*nomos*) or in making people respect the law. A moment ago we called it nomological. It has the force of law, of a law which is the law of the house (*oikos*), of the house as place, domicile, family, lineage, or institution. Having become a museum, Freud's house takes in all these powers of economy.

Two citations will exercise in themselves, in their exergual form, such a function of archival economy. But in making reference to such an economy, an explicit and implicit reference, they will also have this function as theme or as object. These citations concern and bind between themselves, perhaps secretly, two places of *inscription: printing* and *circumcision*.

I

The *first of these exergues* is the more *typographical*. The archive seems here to conform better to its concept. Because it is entrusted to the outside, to an *external* substrate and not, as the sign of the covenant in circumcision, to an *intimate* mark, *right on* the so-called body proper. But where does the outside commence? This question is the question of the archive. There are undoubtedly no others.

At the beginning of chapter 6 of *Civilization and Its Discontents* (1929–30), Freud pretends to worry. Is he not investing in useless expenditure? Is he not in the process of mobilizing a ponderous archiving machine (press, printing, ink, paper) to record something which in the end does not merit such expense? Is not what he is preparing to deliver to the printers so trivial as to be available everywhere? The Freudian lexicon here indeed stresses a certain "printing" technology of archivization (*Eindruck, Druck, drücken*), but only so as to feign the faulty economic calculation. Freud also entrusts to us the "impression" (*Empfindung*), the feeling inspired by this excessive and ultimately gratuitous investment in a perhaps useless archive:

> In none of my previous writings have I had so strong a feeling [*Empfindung*] as now that what I am describing is common knowledge [*allgemein Bekanntes*] and that I am using up paper and ink [*Papier und Tinte*] and, in due course, the compositor's and printer's work and material [*Setzerarbeit und Druckerschwärze aufbieten*] in order to expound things which are, in fact, self-evident [*um eigentlich selbstverständliche Dinge zu erzählen*]. [*SE* 21:117]

In sum, this is a lot of ink and paper for nothing, an entire typographical volume, in short, a material substrate which is out of all proportion, in the last analysis, to "recount" (*erzählen*) stories that everyone knows. But the movement of this rhetoric leads elsewhere. Because Freud draws another inference, in the retrospective logic of a future perfect: *he will have to have invented* an original proposition which will make the investment profitable. In other words, he will have to have found something new *in* psychoanalysis: a mutation or a break within his own theoretical institution. And he will have not only to have announced some news, but also to have archived it: to have put it, as it were, *to the press:*

> For that reason I should be glad to seize the point if it were to appear that the recognition of a special, independent aggressive instinct [*eines besonderen, selbständigen Agressionstriebes*] means an alteration of the psycho-analytic theory of the instincts. [*SE* 21:117]

The rhetoric and the logic of this paragraph are vertiginously cunning. All the more wily because they feign disarmed naïveté. In what can also be read as a theatricalizing of archivization, Freud seems at first to perform a courteous *captatio benevolentiae,* a bit like the one I owe you here: in the end I have nothing new to say. Why detain you with these worn-out stories? Why this wasted time? Why archive this? Why these investments in paper, in ink, in characters? Why mobilize so much space and so much work, so much typographic composition? Does this merit printing? Aren't these stories to be had everywhere?

If it is not without perversity, this *captatio benevolentiae* turns out to be *itself* a useless expenditure, the fiction of a sort of "rhetorical question." Immediately afterward, Freud suggests in effect that this archivization would not be so vain, and a *pure loss,* in the hypothesis that it would cause to appear what in fact he already knows he will cause to appear, and thus this is not a hypothesis for him, a hypothesis submitted for discussion, but rather an irresistible thesis, namely the possibility of a radical perversion, indeed, a diabolical death drive, an aggression or a destruction drive: a drive, thus, of loss. The rest of the chapter recalls everything which had already, since *Beyond the Pleasure Principle* (1920), more than ten years earlier, introduced this destruction drive in the psychic economy, or

| 9

rather the psychic aneconomy, in the accursed share of this pure-loss expenditure. Freud draws the conclusion here with respect to civilization, and indeed to its discontents, while at the same time giving himself over to a sort of autobiographical, theoretical, and institutional anamnesis. In the course of this recapitulation, he stresses above all the resistances that this death drive incites, *everywhere,* outside as much as inside, as it were, and in psychoanalytic circles as well as in himself:

> I remember my own defensive attitude [*meiner eigenen Abwehr*] when the idea of an instinct of destruction first emerged in psycho-analytic literature, and how long it took before I became receptive to it. [*SE* 21:120]

He had previously made two remarks, as if in passing, of which we must not fail to take note. First of all, since overcoming this resistance, he can no longer think otherwise (*ich nicht mehr anders denken kann*). For Sigmund Freud himself, the destruction drive is no longer a debatable hypothesis. Even if this speculation never takes the form of a fixed thesis, even if it is never posited, it is another name for *Anankē,* invincible necessity. It is as if Freud could no longer resist, henceforth, the irreducible and originary perversity of this drive which he names here sometimes death drive, sometimes aggression drive, sometimes destruction drive, as if these three words were in this case synonyms. Second, this three-named drive is mute (*stumm*). It is at work, but since it always operates in silence, it never leaves any archives of its own. It destroys in advance its own archive, as if that were in truth the very motivation of its most proper movement. It works *to destroy the archive: on the condition of effacing* but also *with a view to effacing* its own "proper" traces—which consequently cannot properly be called "proper." It devours it even before producing it on the outside. This drive, from then on, seems not only to be anarchic, anarchontic (we must not forget that the death drive, originary though it may be, is not a principle, as are the pleasure and reality principles): the death drive is above all *anarchivic,* one could say, or *archiviolithic.* It will always have been archive-destroying, by silent vocation.

Allowing for exceptions. But what are exceptions in this case?

Even when it takes the form of an interior desire, the anarchy drive eludes perception, to be sure, save exception: that is, Freud says, except if it disguises itself, except if it tints itself, makes itself up or paints itself (*gefärbt ist*) in some erotic color. This impression of erogenous color draws a mask right on the skin. In other words, the archiviolithic drive is never present in person, neither in itself nor in its effects. It leaves no monument, it bequeaths no document of its own. As inheritance, it leaves only its erotic simulacrum, its pseudonym in painting, its sexual idols, its masks of seduction: lovely impressions. These impressions are perhaps the very origin of what is so obscurely called the beauty of the beautiful. As memories of death.

But, the point must be stressed, this archiviolithic force leaves nothing of its own behind. As the death drive is also, according to the most striking words of Freud himself, an aggression and a destruction (*Destruktion*) drive, it not only incites forgetfulness, amnesia, the annihilation of memory, as *mnēmē* or *anamnēsis,* but also commands the radical effacement, in truth the eradication, of that which can never be reduced to *mnēmē* or to *anamnēsis,* that is, the archive, consignation, the documentary or monumental apparatus as *hypomnēma,* mnemotechnical supplement or representative, auxiliary or memorandum. Because the archive, if this word or this figure can be stabilized so as to take on a signification, will never be either memory or anamnesis as spontaneous, alive and internal experience. On the contrary: the archive takes place at the place of originary and structural breakdown of the said memory.

There is no archive without a place of consignation, without a technique of repetition, and without a certain exteriority. No archive without outside.

Let us never forget this Greek distinction between *mnēmē* or *anamnēsis* on the one hand, and *hypomnēma* on the other. The archive is hypomnesic. And let us note in passing a decisive paradox to which we will not have time to return, but which undoubtedly conditions the whole of these remarks: if there is no archive without consignation in an *external place* which assures the possibility of memorization, of repetition, of reproduction, or of reimpression, then we must also remember that repetition itself, the logic of repetition, indeed the repetition compulsion, remains, according to Freud, indissociable from the death drive. And thus from destruction. Consequence: right on that which permits and conditions archivization, we will never find anything other than that which exposes to destruction, and in truth menaces with destruction, introducing, *a priori,* forgetfulness and the archiviolithic into the heart of the monument. Into the "by heart" itself. The archive always works, and *a priori,* against itself.

The death drive tends thus to destroy the hypomnesic archive, except if it can be disguised, made up, painted, printed, represented as the idol of its truth in painting. Another economy is thus at work, the transaction between this death drive and the pleasure principle, between Thanatos and Eros, but also between the death drive and this apparent dual opposition of principles, of *arkhai,* for example the reality principle and the pleasure principle. The death drive is not a principle. It even threatens every principality, every archontic primacy, every archival desire. It is what we will call, later on, *le mal d'archive,* "archive fever."

Such is the scene, at once within and beyond all staging: Freud can only justify the apparently useless expenditure of paper, ink, and typographic printing, in other words, the laborious investment in the archive, by putting forward the novelty of his discovery, the very one which provokes so much resistance, and first of all in himself, and precisely because its silent vocation is to burn the archive and to incite amnesia, thus refuting the economic principle of the archive, aiming to ruin the archive as accumulation and capitalization of memory on some substrate and in an exterior place.

What, in general, can this substrate consist of? Exterior to what? What does "exterior" mean? Is a circumcision, for example, an exterior mark? Is it an archive?

It *seems* always to be possible, however, to compensate for the aneconomy of this annihilating force allied to the diabolical death drive. This is at least an appearance. Freud, in passing, gives a striking example. At the time of *Discontents* (1929–30), such an example is all the more significant, in its historical and political import. We do not like to be reminded, Freud notes, of the undeniable existence of an evil which seems to contradict the sovereign goodness of God. But if this Devil—another proper name for the three-named drive—seems, then, in the eyes of Christians, for "Christian science" (in English in the text), irreconcilable with God, we see now that it can also exculpate God: evil for evil's sake, diabolical evil, the existence of the Devil can serve as an excuse (*Entschuldigung*) for God, because *exterior* to him, *anarchic angel and dissident,* in rebellion against him, just as, and this is the polemical trait of analogy, the Jew can play the analogous role of economic relief or exoneration (*die selbe ökonomisch entlastende Rolle*) assigned to him by the world of the Aryan ideal. In other words, the radical destruction can again be *reinvested* in another logic, in the inexhaustible *economistic* resource of an archive which capitalizes everything, even that which ruins it or radically contests its power: radical evil can be of service, infinite destruction can be reinvested in a theodicy, the devil can also serve to *justify*—such is the destination of the Jew in the Aryan ideal. (Earlier in the same text, Freud proposes an interesting critique of nationalisms and of anti-Semitism on which we ought to meditate today but which we cannot possibly enter into here.)

In a preliminary fashion, and still limiting ourselves to this archivization of the Freudian archive, we ought to pay attention also to a date. Let us consider the technical model of the machine tool, intended, in Freud's eyes, to *represent on the outside* memory as *internal* archivization, namely the *Mystic Pad* (*der Wunderblock*). This model was also described, analyzed, presented after *Beyond the Pleasure Principle,* the book in which Freud admits to playing *"the devil's advocate."* The description includes several allusions to that which in the functioning of this *Mystic Pad* is conditioned by the earlier description, in *Beyond,* of the structure of the psychic apparatus. In translating and questioning this strange *Notiz über den Wunderblock,* I attempted long ago to analyze, as closely as possible, the relations between the model of archivization, technicality, time, and death. I tried to delimit the thinking this text engendered from within the metaphysical assurances in which, it seems to me, it is held. Without recalling here the questions I formulated at the time (in particular concerning the "Freudian concept of the hereditary mnemic trace" [*Writing and Difference* 197; *L'écriture* 294]), I would simply like to cite one comment. It sketched, by anticipation, the horizon I hope to follow more closely and differently tonight. To represent the functioning of the psychic apparatus in an *exterior* technical model, Freud did not have at his disposition the resources provided today by archival machines of which one could hardly have dreamed in the first quarter of this century. Do these new archival machines change anything? Do they affect the essentials of Freud's discourse? In 1966, I noted the following (forgive me for this long citation, I will not allow myself any others):

> [T]he Mystic Pad, separated from psychical responsibility, a representation abandoned to itself, still participates in Cartesian space and mechanics: *natural* wax, exteriority of the *memory aid.*
>
> All that Freud had thought about the unity of life and death, however, should have led him to ask other questions here. And to ask them explicitly. Freud does not explicitly examine the status of the "materialized" supplement which is necessary to the alleged spontaneity of memory, even if that spontaneity were differentiated in itself, thwarted by a censorship or repression which, moreover, could not act on a perfectly spontaneous memory. Far from the machine being a pure absence of spontaneity, its *resemblance* to the psychical apparatus, its existence and its necessity bear witness to the finitude of the mnemic spontaneity which is thus supplemented. The machine—and, consequently, representation—is death and finitude *within* the psyche. Nor does Freud examine the possibility of this machine, which, in the world, has at least begun to *resemble* memory, and increasingly resembles it more closely. Its resemblance to memory is closer than that of the innocent Mystic Pad: the latter is no doubt infinitely more complex than slate or paper, less archaic than a palimpsest; but, compared to other machines for storing archives, it is a child's toy. [*Writing and Difference* 227–28; *L'écriture* 336–37]

What is at issue here is nothing less than the *future,* if there is such a thing: the future of psychoanalysis in its relation to the future of science. As techno-science, science, in its very movement, can only consist in a transformation of the techniques of archivization, of printing, of inscription, of reproduction, of formalization, of ciphering, and of translating marks.

The questions which now arise are of at least *two orders.*

1. Those of the first engage the *theoretical exposition* of psychoanalysis. They would concern its *object,* and in particular all that is invested in the representational models of the psychic apparatus as an apparatus for perception, for printing, for recording, for topic distribution of places of inscription, of ciphering, of repression, of displacement, of condensation. These are our names for as many places of reading and interpretation, needless to say—and this is why the field of these questions is not properly a field. It can no longer be delimited. Independently of the reservations I had formulated in "Freud and the Scene of Writing" about the presuppositions of modeling itself (reservations I will not return to here), it is at least possible to ask whether, *concerning the essentials, and beyond the extrinsic details,* the structure of the psychic apparatus, this system, at once mnesic and hypomnesic, which Freud sought to describe with the "mystic pad," resists the evolution of archival technoscience or not. Is the psychic apparatus *better represented* or is it *affected differently* by all the technical mechanisms for archivization and for reproduction, for prostheses of so-called live memory, for simulacrums of living things which already are, and will increasingly be, more refined, complicated, powerful than the "mystic pad" (microcomputing, electronization, computerization, etc.)?

Neither of these hypotheses can be reduced to the other. Because if the upheavals in progress affected the very structures of the psychic apparatus, for example in their spatial architecture and in their economy of speed, in their processing of spacing and of temporalization, it would be a question no longer of simple continuous progress in representation, in the *representative* value of the model, but rather of an entirely different logic.

2. Other related questions, but of another order: they concern no longer only the theoretical object of psychoanalysis in its exposition, but rather the archivization of psychoanalysis itself, of its "life," if you will, of its *"acts,"* of its private and public procedures,

those which are secret or manifest, provisionally or definitively encrypted; they concern the archivization of its institutional and clinical practice, of the academic, scientific, and juridico-editorial aspect of the immense problems of publication or of translation with which we are acquainted. The word "acts" can designate here at once the content of what is to be archived *and* the archive itself, the archivable and the archiving of the archive: the printed and the printing of impression. Whether it is a question of the private or public life of Freud, of his partners or of his inheritors, sometimes also of his patients, of the personal or scientific exchanges, of the letters, deliberations, or politico-institutional decisions, of the practices and of their rules (for example, those of the so-called "analytic situation," the place and the length of the sessions, association which is free, oral, in person, and in the presence of the analyst, without technical recording), in what way has the whole of this field been determined by a state of the technology of communication and of archivization? One can dream or speculate about the geo-techno-logical shocks which would have made the landscape of the psychoanalytic archive unrecognizable for the past century if, to limit myself to these indications, Freud, his contemporaries, collaborators and immediate disciples, instead of writing thousands of letters by hand, had had access to MCI or AT&T telephonic credit cards, portable tape recorders, computers, printers, faxes, televisions, teleconferences, and above all E-mail.

I would have liked to devote my whole lecture to this retrospective science fiction. I would have liked to imagine with you the scene of that other archive after the earthquake and after the *"après-coups"* of its aftershocks. This is indeed where we are. As I am not able to do this, on account of the still archaic organization of our colloquia, of the time and the space at our disposal, I will limit myself to a mechanical remark: this archival earthquake would not have limited its effects to the *secondary recording,* to the printing and to the conservation of the history of psychoanalysis. It would have transformed this history from top to bottom and in the most initial inside of its production, in its very *events.* This is another way of saying that the archive, as printing, writing, prosthesis, or hypomnesic technique in general is not only the place for stocking and for conserving an archivable content *of the past* which would exist in any case, such as, without the archive, one still believes it was or will have been. No, the technical structure of the *archiving* archive also determines the structure of the *archivable* content even in its very coming into existence and in its relationship to the future. The archivization produces as much as it records the event. This is also our political experience of the so-called news media.

This means that, *in the past,* psychoanalysis would not have been what it was (any more than so many other things) if E-mail, for example, had existed. And *in the future* it will no longer be what Freud and so many psychoanalysts have anticipated, from the moment E-mail, for example, became possible. One could find many clues other than E-mail. As a postal technology, the example undoubtedly merits some privilege. First of all because of the major and exceptional role (exceptional in the history of scientific projects) played at the center of the psychoanalytic archive by a handwritten correspondence. We have yet to finish discovering and processing this immense corpus, in part unpublished, in part secret, and perhaps in part radically and irreversibly destroyed—for example by Freud himself. Who knows? One must consider the historical and nonaccidental reasons which have tied such an institution, in its theoretical and practical dimensions, to postal communication and to this particular form of mail, to its substrates, to its average speed: a handwritten letter takes so many days to arrive in another European city, and nothing is ever independent of this delay. Everything remains on its scale.

But the example of E-mail is privileged in my opinion for a more important and obvious reason: because electronic mail today, even more than the fax, is on the way to transforming the entire public and private space of humanity, and first of all the limit between the private, the secret (private or public), and the public or the phenomenal. It is not only a technique, in the ordinary and limited sense of the term: at an unprecedented rhythm, in quasi-instantaneous fashion, this instrumental possibility of production, of printing, of conservation, and of destruction of the archive must inevitably be accompanied by juridical and thus political transformations. These affect nothing less than property rights, publishing and reproduction rights. In regard to and in keeping with the dimension of these transformations under way, these radical and interminable turbulences, we must take stock today of the classical works which continue in the beehive of Freudian studies—concerning the manuscripts of Freud and of his intimates, the published and still-unpublished correspondence, the publications or re-publications, the drafts and the sketches, the accessible and the inaccessible, the notorious filterings of the Library of Congress, etc. These classical and extraordinary works move away from us at great speed, in a continually accelerated fashion. They burrow into the past at a distance more and more comparable to that which separates us from archaeological digs (that bizarre activity talked about by the author of *Gradiva,* to which we will be turning shortly), from biblical philology, from the translations of the Bible, from Luther to Rozenweig or to Buber, or from the establishing of the hypomnesic writings of Plato or of Aristotle by medieval copyists. This is another way to say that it takes nothing away from the admirable nobility, from the indisputable necessity, and from the incontestable legitimacy of this classical philology which is so much more than philology. But this should not close our eyes to the unlimited upheaval under way in archival technology. It should above all remind us that the said archival technology no longer determines, will never have determined, merely the moment of the conservational recording, but rather the very institution of the archivable event. It conditions not only the form or the structure that prints, but the printed content of the printing: the *pressure* of the *printing,* the *impression,* before the division between the printed and the printer. This archival technique has commanded that which in the past even instituted and constituted whatever there was as anticipation of the future.

And as wager [*gageure*]. The archive has always been a *pledge,* and like every pledge [*gage*], a token of the future. To put it more trivially: what is no longer archived in the same way is no longer lived in the same way. Archivable meaning is also and in advance codetermined by the structure that archives. It begins with the printer.

We shall leave these questions suspended for the moment. Let us simply remark, and this is the same concern for the archive, a dating: this "mystic pad," this *exterior,* thus archival, model of the *psy-*

chic recording and memorization apparatus, does not only integrate the inaugural concepts of psychoanalysis, from the *Sketches* up to the articles of the *Metapsychology,* by way of the *Traumdeutung,* in particular all those which concern for example repression, censorship, recording (*Niederschrift*) in the two systems (Ucs and Pcs), the three points of view (topic, dynamic, and economic). Taking into account the multiplicity of regions *in* the psychic apparatus, this model also integrates the necessity, inside the *psyche* itself, of a certain outside, of certain borders between insides and outsides. And with this *domestic outside,* that is to say also with the hypothesis of an *internal* substrate, surface, or space without which there is neither consignation, registration, impression nor suppression, censorship, repression, it prepares the idea of a psychic archive distinct from spontaneous memory, of a *hypomnēsis* distinct from *mnēmē* and from *anamnēsis:* the institution, in sum, of a *prosthesis of the inside.* We have said "institution" (one could say "erection") so as to mark, right from the originary threshold of this prosthesis, a rupture which is just as originary with nature. The theory of psychoanalysis, then, becomes a theory of the archive and not only a theory of memory. This does not prevent the Freudian discourse from remaining heterogeneous, as I tried to show in "Freud and the Scene of Writing": an antagonistic and traditional motif continues in this discourse to oppose a metaphysics to the rigorous consequence of this prosthetics, that is, of a logic of hypomnesis.

The model of this singular *"mystic pad"* also incorporates what may seem, in the form of a destruction drive, to contradict even the conservation drive, what we could call here the *archive drive.* It is what I called earlier, and in view of this internal contradiction, *archive fever.* There would indeed be no archive desire without the radical finitude, without the possibility of a forgetfulness which does not limit itself to repression. Above all, and this is the most serious, beyond or within this simple limit called finiteness or finitude, there is no archive fever without the threat of this death drive, this aggression and destruction drive. This threat is *in-finite,* it sweeps away the logic of finitude and the simple factual limits, the transcendental aesthetics, one might say, the spatio-temporal conditions of conservation. Let us rather say that it abuses them. Such an abuse opens the ethico-political dimension of the problem.

There is not one archive fever, one limit or one suffering of memory among others: enlisting the in-finite, archive fever verges on radical evil.

II

Let us encrust a second citation into the exergue. Less typographical than the first, as we said, it nonetheless still maintains a reference to the *graphic* mark and to repetition, indeed to printing of the *typical* sort. Recurrent and iterable, it carries literal singularity into figurality. Again inscribing inscription, it commemorates in its way, effectively, a circumcision. A very singular monument, it is also the document of an archive. In a reiterated manner, it leaves the trace of an incision *right on* the skin: more than one skin, at more than one age. To the letter or by figure. The foliaceous stratification, the pellicular superimposition of these cutaneous marks seems to defy analysis. It accumulates so many sedimented archives, some of which are written right on the epidermis of a body proper, others on the substrate of an "exterior" body. Each layer here seems to gape slightly, as the lips of a wound, permitting glimpses of the abyssal possibility of another depth destined for archaeological excavation.

It has, in appearance, primarily to do with a *private inscription*. This is the title of a first problem concerning the question of its belonging to an archive: which archive? that of Sigmund Freud? that of the psychoanalytic institution or science? Where does one draw the limit? What is this new science of which the institutional and theoretical archive ought by rights to comprise the most private documents, sometimes secret? beginning with those of its presumed founder, its arch-father, its patriarch, Freud? Indeed, of the arch-patriarch, Sigmund's father, Jakob? This brings us to the question, which is always open, of what the title "Freud's house" means, the Freud Museum as a "House of Freud," the *arkheion* of which we are the guests, *in* which we speak, *from* which we speak. *To* which we speak, I might also say: addressing it. The archive of the singular private inscription I will speak of has been in the public domain for several years. One can have access to it in several languages, beginning with its original in Hebrew. Public, and offered for interpretation, this document is henceforth accompanied, indissociably, by an extraordinary exegetical or hermeneutic apparatus.

It is an inscription in the form of a dedication. It was written by the hand of Jakob, son of R. Shelomoh Freud, the arch-patriarch, the grandfather of psychoanalysis, and addressed to his son, Shelomoh Sigmund Freud, on the day of his thirty-fifth birthday, in Vienna, the sixth of May, 1891 (29 Nisan 5651).

A gift *carried* this inscription. What the father gives to the son is at once a writing and its substrate. The substrate, in a sense, was the Bible itself, the "Book of books," a Philippsohn Bible Sigmund had studied in his youth. His father restores it to him, after having made a present of it to him; he restitutes it as a gift, with a new leather binding. To bind anew: this is an act of love. Of paternal love. It is no less important than the text in *melitzah,* those biblical, liturgical, or rabbinical fragments which compose the long dedication and carry in turn the thoughts of the father. On this subject he speaks of a "new skin," as the English translation of the Hebrew says.

Like some of you, I suppose, I discovered the treasure of this archive, illuminated by a new translation and by an original interpretation, in Yosef Hayim Yerushalmi's handsome book *Freud's Moses: Judaism Terminable and Interminable.* This book left a strong impression on me. My recent discovery of it gave me much to think about, more than I could say here, and it has accompanied the preparation of this lecture. So this lecture will naturally be dedicated, if he will allow it, to Yosef Hayim Yerushalmi.[2] For a reason that will perhaps become clear later, I will dare to dedicate it at the same time to my sons—and even to the memory of my father, who was also called, as is life itself, Hayim.

Here is the archived dedication that the grandfather or the arch-patriarch of psychoanalysis, Jakob Freud, inscribed on the Bible he gave, but in truth returned, *sous peau neuve* ["under new skin"], as they say in French, to his son, that is, to the father or the patriarch of psychoanalysis. Yerushalmi cites it with dramatic effect, as a *coup*

2. Yerushalmi, who participated in this conference, was to have been at this lecture. As he was sick, he could not be present, and his own contribution was read by someone else the next day.

de théâtre, at the end of his book, just before the other dramatic effect of an audacious fiction, the extraordinary "Monologue with Freud," to which I will return at length. He sees in this dedication "one crucial episode," and he speaks of "the one canonical text of Jakob Freud at our disposal" [70].

So this is not just any archive and just any moment in the history of the archive. Later, beyond this exergue, we will see how Yerushalmi presents the character, to his eyes properly inaugural, of the discovery, of the reading, and of the establishment of this "crucial" archive of which he is in sum the first guardian, the first reader, the first doctor, indeed the only legitimate archon.

In the body of this inscription, we must at least underline all the words that point, indeed, toward the institution and the tradition of the law ("lawmakers"), that is to say, toward that archontic dimension without which one could not have archives, but also, more directly, toward the logic and the semantics of the archive, of memory and of the memorial, of conservation and of inscription which put into reserve ("store"), accumulate, capitalize, stock a quasi-infinity of layers, of archival strata that are at once superimposed, overprinted, and enveloped in each other. To read, in this case, requires working at geological or archaeological excavations, on substrates or under surfaces, old or new skins, the hypermnesic and hypomnesic epidermises of books or penises—and the very first sentence recalls, at least by figure,[3] the circumcision of the father of psychoanalysis, "in the seventh in the days of the years of your life." I will cite the translation given by Yerushalmi while un-

---

22

3. I decided I should make this prudent addition ("at least by figure") after a friendly talk with Yerushalmi, who, several months later in New York, correctly warned me against a reading which would seem to identify here a *literal* or *direct* reference to the dated event of a circumcision. I see it as he does and am more clearly aware of it today thanks to him. This is yet another reason for my gratitude. As it seems nonetheless difficult to contest that this dedication in *melitzah* gathers all its signs and makes all its figures (beginning with that of the "new skin") converge toward the moment of a covenant, in truth of a renewed covenant, is it improper to read here an anniversary recall, by a father to a son, of circumcision? That is, of the very figure of the covenant, in its *typical* moment, in the type of an incisive inscription, in its *character,* at once inaugural and recurrent, regularly renewed?

derlining a few words, and then I will abandon this exergue, to which I will return later:

Son who is dear to me, Shelomoh. In the *seventh in the days* of the years of your life the Spirit of the Lord began to move you and spoke within you: Go, read my Book that I have written and there will burst open for you the wellsprings of understanding, knowledge, and wisdom. Behold, it is the Book of Books, from which sages have *excavated* and *lawmakers* learned knowledge and judgement. A vision of the Almighty did you see; you heard and strove to do, and you soared on the wings of the Spirit.

Since then the book has been *stored* like the fragments of the tablets in an *ark with me.* For the day on which your years were filled to five and thirty I have put upon it *a cover of new skin* and have called it: "Spring up, O well, sing ye unto it!" And I have presented it to you as *a memorial and as a reminder* [a memorial and a reminder, the one and the other at once, the one in the other, and we have, perhaps, in the economy of these two words the whole of archival law: *anamnēsis, mnēmē, hypomnēma*] of love from your father, who loves you with everlasting love.

Jakob son of R. Shelomoh Freid [sic]
In the capital city Vienna 29 Nisan [5]651 6 May [1]891 [71]

Arch-archive, the book was "stored" *with* the arch-patriarch of psychoanalysis. It was stored there in the Ark of the Covenant [Deut. 10:1–5]. *Arca,* this time in Latin, is the chest, the "ark of acacia wood," which contains the stone Tablets; but *arca* is also the cupboard, the coffin, the prison cell, or the cistern, the reservoir.[4]

4. The ark stays *with* the father of the father of psychoanalysis. Stay with me, Jahveh had said to Moses, send them to their tents [5: 30–31]. Shortly after the reminder of the Ark of the Covenant figures the order to circumcise the foreskin of the heart [10:16].

P r e a m b l e

I undoubtedly owe you, at the beginning of this preamble, a first explication concerning the word *impression,* which risks, in my title, being somewhat enigmatic. I became aware of this afterward: when Elisabeth Roudinesco asked me on the telephone for a provisional title, so as indeed to send the program of this conference to press, almost a year before inscribing and printing on my computer the first word of what I am saying to you here, the response I then improvised ended up in effect imposing the word *impression.*

And in an instant, it was as if *three meanings* had condensed themselves and overprinted each other from the back of my memory. Which were they?

Without waiting, I have spoken to you of my computer, of the little portable Macintosh on which I have begun to write. For it has not only been the first substrate to support all of these words. On a beautiful morning in California a few weeks ago, I asked myself a certain question, among so many others. Without being able to find a response, while reading on the one hand Freud, on the other Yerushalmi, and while tinkling away on my computer. I asked myself what is the moment *proper* to the archive, if there is such a thing, the instant of archivization strictly speaking, which is not, and I will come back to this, so-called live or spontaneous memory (*mnēmē or anamnēsis*), but rather a certain hypomnesic and prosthetic experience of the technical substrate. Was it not at this very instant that, having written something or other on the screen, the letters remaining as if suspended and floating yet at the surface of a liquid element, I pushed a certain key to "save" a text undamaged, in a hard and lasting way, to protect marks from being erased, so as to ensure in this way salvation and *indemnity,* to stock, to accumulate, and, in what is at once the same thing and something else, to make the sentence available in this way for printing and for reprinting, for reproduction? Does it change anything that Freud did not know about the computer? And where should the moment of suppression or of repression be situated in these new models of recording and impression, or printing?

This condensation of three meanings of the word "impression" was only able to imprint itself in me in a single stroke, apparently in an instant of no duration, after much work, discontinuous though it may have been, with Freud's texts, with certain of his writings, but also with themes, with figures, with conceptual schemes that are familiar to me to the point of obsession and yet remain no less secret, young, and still to come for me: writing, the trace, inscription, on an exterior substrate or on the so-called body proper, as for example, and this is not just any example for me, that singular and immemorial archive called *circumcision,* and which, though never leaving you, nonetheless has come about, and is no less exterior, *exterior right on* your body proper.

So what are these *three meanings* which, in a single instant, condensed themselves and overprinted each other, that is to say overdetermined each other, in the word "impression" and the phrase "Freudian impression"? And above all, of course, in their relationship to that re-producible, iterable, and conservative production of memory, to that objectivizable storage called the archive?

26   1. The first impression is *scriptural* or *typographic:* that of an inscription (*Niederschrift,* says Freud throughout his works) which leaves a mark at the surface or in the thickness of a substrate. And in any case, directly or indirectly, this concept—or rather this *figure* of the substrate—marks the properly *fundamental* assignation of our problem, the problem of the fundamental. Can one imagine an archive without foundation, without substrate, without sub-

stance, without subjectile? And if it were impossible, what of the history of substrates? What of the future of the substrate in its relationship to the history of psychoanalysis? From the *Sketches* up to *Beyond,* to the *Mystic Pad* and beyond, there is no limit to this problematic of the impresson, that is, of the inscription, which leaves a mark right on the substrate. This then becomes a place of consignation, of "inscription" or of "recording," as the *Metapsychology* frequently says (*"Niederlassung oder Niederschrift,"* "installation," "location or registration") when it recalls, for example in *The Unconscious,* at least three things:

a. the topological hypothesis of several psychological systems ("two or three")—thus what permits one to justify the distinction between memory and archive—explains why psychoanalysis was spoken of, and in part incorrectly, as a "depth-psychology" or an *"abyssal psychology"* (*Tiefenpsychologie*) [*SE* 14:173];

b. this topic has nothing to do, for the moment, at this time, *"for the present"* (underlined by Freud), with an anatomical point of view on cerebral localizations. By stressing in italics *"for the present"* (*vorläufig*), Freud clearly wants to leave room for what the future of science may teach us about this;

c. lastly, these hypotheses are nothing other, and nothing more than, intuitive representations (*Veranschaulichungen*), "graphic illustrations" according to the English translation. They "set out to be no more than graphic illustrations" [*SE* 14:175]

This problematic of impression is discouraging for those who might wish to find in it a privileged entrance. Because it becomes confused with the whole corpus of Freud's works, whether it has to do with collective or individual memory, with censorship or repression, with dynamic, with topic, or with economy, with the Ucs or Pcs systems, with perception, with mnesic trace.

It is undoubtedly because I had already privileged it, in many other texts, that this typographic figure of the press, of printing, or of the imprint imposed itself so quickly on me over the telephone with the word "impression." This word capitalizes on a double advantage, above all in a country of English-speaking culture. In the first place, it reawakens the code of English empiricism: the concepts of sensible "impression" and of copy play a major role there in the genealogy of ideas; and is not the copy of an impression already a sort of archive? In the second place, the word "impression" reminds us that no tunnel in history will ever align the two translations of *Verdrängung:* "repression" in English, as in Spanish, a word that belongs to the same family as "impression" (the *Verdrängung* always represses an impression), and *refoulement* in French, a word that is not allied to the semantic family of the "impression," as is the word *répression,* which we reserve in French for the translation of *Unterdrückung,* most often translated in English, as in Spanish and Portuguese, by "supression."

The stakes of this conceptual difference between *Verdrängung* and *Unterdrückung* are not limited to nominal questions of translation, of rhetoric or of semantics, although they are also accumulated there. They directly concern the structures of archivization. Because they touch on the topic differences and thus on the location of the substrates of traces, on the subjectile of consignation (*Niederschrift*), from one system to the other. Unlike repression (*Verdrängung*), which remains unconscious in its operation and in its result, suppression (*Unterdrückung*) effects what Freud calls a "second censorship"—between the conscious and the preconscious—or rather affects the affect, which is to say, that which *can never* be repressed in the unconscious but only suppressed and displaced in another affect.

It is one of the numerous questions we will not be able to treat here. In their epistemology, in their historiography, in their operations as well as in their object, what should the classical archivists or historians make of this distinction between "repression" and *répression,* between *Verdrängung* and *Unterdrückung,* between "repression" and "suppression"? If this distinction has any relevance, it will be enough to disrupt the tranquil landscape of all historical knowledge, of all historiography, and even of all self-consistent "scholarship." Who could say that this has only begun to happen? And even among the historians of psychoanalysis, who nevertheless ought to be the first to rework their axiomatics and their methodology, even assuming that the classical concept of historical science and of "scholarship" still resists and rides out this mutation intact?

2. This orients us toward the second valence of the word "impression." It no doubt seems less immediately necessary and obvious. "Impression," "Freudian impression": this no doubt made something else be felt in anticipation. What?

Well, concerning the archive, Freud never managed to form anything that deserves to be called a concept. Neither have we, by the way. We have no concept, only an impression, a series of impressions associated with a word. To the rigor of the *concept,* I am opposing here the vagueness or the open imprecision, the relative indetermination of such a *notion.* "Archive" is only a *notion,* an impression associated with a word and for which, together with Freud, we do not have a concept. We only have an impression, an insistent impression through the unstable feeling of a shifting figure, of a schema, or of an in-finite or indefinite process. Unlike what a classical philosopher or scholar would be tempted to do, I do not consider this impression, or the notion of this impression, to be a subconcept, the feebleness of a blurred and subjective pre-knowledge, destined for I know not what sin of nominalism, but to the contrary, as I will explain later, I consider it to be the possibility and the very future of the concept, to be the very concept of the future, if there is such a thing and if, as I believe, the idea of the archive depends on it. This is one of the theses: there are essential reasons for which a concept in the process of being formed always remains inadequate relative to what it ought to be, divided, disjointed between two forces. And this disjointedness has a necessary relationship with the structure of archivization.

It follows, certainly, that Freudian psychoanalysis proposes a new theory of the archive; it takes into account a topic and a death drive without which there would not in effect be any desire or any possibility for the archive. But at the same time, at once for strategic reasons and because the conditions of archivization implicate all the tensions, contradictions, or aporias we are trying to formalize here, notably those which make it into a movement of the promise and of the future no less than of recording the past, the concept of the archive must inevitably carry in itself, as does every concept, an unknowable weight. The presupposition of this weight also takes on the *figures* of "repression" and "suppression," even if it cannot necessarily be reduced to these. This double presupposition leaves an imprint. It inscribes an impression in language and in discourse. The unknowable weight that imprints itself thus does not weigh only as a negative charge. It involves the history of the concept, it inflects archive desire or fever, their opening on the future, their dependency with respect to what will come, in short, all that ties knowledge and memory to the promise.

3. "Freudian impression" also has a third meaning, unless it is the first: the impression *left* by Sigmund Freud, beginning with the impression *left* in him, inscribed in him, from his birth and his covenant, from his circumcision, through all the manifest or secret history of psychoanalysis, of the institution and of the works, by way of the public and private correspondence, including this letter from Jakob Shelomoh Freid to Shelomoh Sigmund Freud in memory of the signs or tokens of the covenant and to accompany the "new skin" of a Bible. I wish to speak of the *impression left* by Freud, by the event which carries this family name, the nearly unforgettable and incontestable, undeniable *impression* (even and above all for those who deny it) that Sigmund Freud will have *made* on anyone, after him, who speaks *of him* or speaks *to him,* and who must then, accepting it or not, knowing it or not, be thus marked: in his or her culture and discipline, whatever it may be, in particular philosophy, medicine, psychiatry, and more precisely here, because we are speaking of memory and of archive, the history of texts and of discourses, political history, legal history, the history of ideas or of culture, the history of religion and religion itself, the history of institutions and of sciences, in particular the history of this institutional and scientific project called psychoanalysis. Not to mention the history of history, the history of historiography. In any given discipline, one can no longer, one should no longer be able to, thus one no longer has the right or the means to claim to speak of this without having been marked in advance, in one way or another, by this Freudian impression. It is impossible and illegitimate to do so without having integrated, well or badly, in an important way or not, recognizing it or denying it, what is here called the *Freudian impression.* If one is under the impression

that it is possible not to take this into account, forgetting it, effacing it, crossing it out, or objecting to it, one has already confirmed, we could even say countersigned (thus archived), a "repression" or a "suppression." This, then, is perhaps what I heard without hearing, what I understood without understanding, what I wanted obscurely to overhear, allowing these words to dictate to me over the telephone, in "Freudian impression."

F o r e w o r d

It is thus our impression that we can no longer ask the question of the concept, of the history of the concept, and notably of the concept of the archive. No longer, at least, in a temporal or historical modality dominated by the present or by the past. We no longer feel we have the right to ask questions whose form, grammar, and lexicon nonetheless seem so legitimate, sometimes so neutral. We no longer find assured meaning in questions such as these: do we *already* have at our disposition a concept of the archive? a concept of the archive which deserves this name? which is one and whose unity is assured? Have we ever been assured of the homogeneity, of the consistency, of the univocal relationship of any concept to a term or to such a word as "archive"?

In their form and in their grammar, these questions are all turned toward the past: they ask if we *already* have at our disposal such a concept and if we have ever had any assurance in this regard. To have a concept at one's disposal, to have assurances with regard to it, is to presuppose a closed heritage and the guarantee sealed, in some sense, by that heritage. And the word and the notion of the archive seem at first, admittedly, to point toward the past, to refer to the signs of consigned memory, to recall faithfulness to tradition. If we have attempted to underline the past in these questions from the outset, it is also to indicate the direction of another problematic. As much as and more than a thing of the past, before such a thing, the archive should *call into question* the coming of the future. And if we still lack a viable, unified, given concept of the archive, it is undoubtedly not a purely conceptual, theoretical, epistemological insufficiency on the level of multiple and specific disciplines; it is perhaps not for lack of sufficient elucidation in certain circumscribed domains: archaeology, documentography, bibliography, philology, historiography.

Let us imagine in effect a project of general archiviology, a word that does not exist but that could designate a general and interdisciplinary science of the archive. Such a discipline must in effect risk being paralyzed in a preliminary aporia. It would have *either* (1) to include psychoanalysis, a scientific project which, as one could easily show, aspires to be a general science of the archive, of everything that can happen to the economy of memory and to its substrates, traces, documents, in their supposedly psychical or techno-prosthetic forms (internal or external: the mystic pads of the past or of the future, what they represent and what they supplement), *or* (2) on the contrary, to place itself under the *critical* authority (in the Kantian sense) of psychoanalysis, continue to dispute it, of course, but after having integrated its logic, its concepts, its metapsychology, its economy, its topic, etc., as Freud repeats them again in such precise fashion in the third part of his *Moses,* when he treats at length the "difficulties," the archival problems of oral narrative and public property, of mnesic traces, of archaic and transgenerational heritage, and of everything that can happen to an "impression" in these at once "topic" (*topisch*) and "genetic" (*genetisch*) processes. He repeats here that this topic has nothing to do with the anatomy of the brain, and this is enough to complicate the phylogenetic dimension, which he judges to be in effect irreducible but which he is far from simplifying in its Lamarckian schemas (he is often accused of this, by Yerushalmi also), or even its Darwinian ones. The adherence to a biological doctrine of acquired characters—of the biological archive, in sum—cannot be made to agree in a simple and immediate way with all Freud acknowledges otherwise: the memory of the experience of previous generations, the time of the formation of languages and of a symbolicity that transcends given languages and discursivity as such. Freud is careful. He knows and recognizes explicitly "the present attitude of biological science, which refuses to hear of the inheritance of acquired characters by succeeding generations" [*Moses and Monotheism, SE* 23:100].[5] And if he admits that it is difficult for him to do without a reference to biological evolution (and who could seriously reproach him for that, in principle and absolutely? in the name of what?), he shows himself in this regard to be more reserved and more circumspect than is usually acknowledged, distinguishing notably between acquired characters ("which are hard to grasp") and "memory-traces of external events" [*SE* 23:100]. These characters and these traces could well follow (Freud would certainly not say it here in this form) quite complicated linguistic, cultural, cipherable, and in general ciphered transgenerational and transindividual relays, transiting thus through an archive, the science of which is not at a standstill. This does not necessarily bring us back to Lamarck or to Darwin, even if it obliges us to articulate the history of genetic programs and ciphers on all the symbolic and individual archives differently. All that Freud says is that we are receptive to an analogy between the two types of transgenerational memory or archive (the memory of an ancestral experience or the so-called biologically acquired character) and that "we cannot imagine [*vorstellen*] one without the other" [*SE* 23:100]. Without the irrepressible, that is to say, only suppressible and repressible, force and authority of this transgenerational memory, the problems of which we speak would be dissolved and resolved in advance. There would no longer be any essential history of culture, there would no longer be any question of memory and of archive, of

5. Yerushalmi takes these texts into account. He is well aware that Freud was well aware of it: the inheritance of acquired characters was contested by science. To explain a nonetheless obstinate predilection for Lamarckism, he evokes the precious works of Ilse Grubrich-Simitis on this subject, then asks himself if Lamarckism (without of course being something "Jewish") did not tempt the Jew in Freud. "Deconstructed into Jewish terms," does Lamarckism not signify that the Jew cannot cease being Jewish "because one's fate in being Jewish was determined long ago by the Fathers, and that often what one feels most deeply and obscurely is a trilling wire in the blood" [31]? A letter from Freud to Zweig speaks the same language, in effect, concerning the land of Israel and the heritage that centuries of inhabitation have perhaps left in "our blood and nerves" [qtd. in Yerushalmi 31]. Yerushalmi also cites Edelheit in an note: for Freud, in effect, "although human evolution is 'Darwinian via the genes' it is 'Lamarckian via language and culture'" [31n44].

patriarchive or of matriarchive, and one would no longer even understand how an ancestor can speak within us, nor what sense there might be in us to speak *to* him or her, to speak in such an *unheimlich,* "uncanny" fashion, to his or her ghost. *With* it.

We have already encountered this alternative, we will return to it again: Must one apply to what will have been predefined as the Freudian or psychoanalytic archive in general schemas of reading, of interpretation, of classification which have been received and reflected out of this corpus whose unity is thus presupposed? Or rather, has one on the contrary the right to treat the said psychoanalytico-Freudian archive according to a logic or a method, a historiography or a hermeneutic independent of Freudian psychoanalysis, indeed anterior even to the very name of Freud, while presupposing in another manner the closure and the identity of this corpus? This independence can take numerous forms, pre- or postpsychoanalytic, with or without an explicit project: to integrate and to formalize what a minute ago we called the Freudian impression. This is an experience familiar to a number of those who are participating in this conference or who share this concern, and not only, here and there, to the most eminent historians of psychoanalysis.

In an enigmatic sense, which will clarify itself *perhaps* (perhaps, because nothing should be sure here, for essential reasons), the question of the archive is not, we repeat, a question of the past. It is not the question of a concept dealing with the past that might *already* be at our disposal or not at our disposal, *an archivable concept of the archive.* It is a question of the future, the question of the future itself, the question of a response, of a promise and of a responsibility for tomorrow. The archive: if we want to know what that will have meant, we will only know in times to come. Perhaps. Not tomorrow but in times to come, later on or perhaps never. A spectral messianicity is at work in the concept of the archive and ties it, like religion, like history, like science itself, to a very singular experience of the promise. And we are never far from Freud in saying this. Messianicity does not mean messianism. Having explained myself on this elsewhere, in *Specters of Marx,* and even if this distinction remains fragile and enigmatic, allow me to treat it as established, in order to save time.

Later, we ought, perhaps, to formulate the concept and the formal law of this messianic hypothesis. For the moment, allow me to illustrate it while evoking again one of the most striking moments in the scene, if I may say it in front of him, that Yerushalmi has with Freud, at the end of his book, in what he calls his "Monologue with Freud." We must come to the moment at which Yerushalmi seems to suspend everything, in particular everything he has said and done up to this point, from the thread of a discrete sentence. One could be tempted to regard this thread as the umbilical cord of the book. Everything seems to be suspended from this umbilical cord—by the umbilical cord of the event which such a book as this represents. For in a work entirely devoted to memory and to the archive, a sentence on the last page says the future. It says, in the future tense: "Much will depend, of course, on how the very terms *Jewish* and *science* are to be defined" [100]. This sentence followed an allusion to "much future work," and it aggravated the opening of this future, enlarging it accordingly, in which the *very possibility of knowledge* remained suspended in the conditional:

> Professor Freud, at this point I find it futile to ask whether, genetically or structurally, psychoanalysis is really a Jewish science; that we shall know, *if it is at all knowable,* only when much future work has been done. Much will depend, of course, on how the very terms *Jewish* and *science* are to be defined. [100, my emphasis]

Dramatic turn, stroke of theater, *coup de théâtre* within *coup de théâtre*. In an instant which dislocates the linear order of presents, a second *coup de théâtre* illuminates the first. It is also the thunderbolt of love at first sight, a *coup de foudre* (love and transference) which, in a flash, transfixes with light the memory of the first. With another light. One no longer knows what the *time,* what the *tense* of this theater will have been, the first stroke of *theater,* the first *stroke,* the *first.* The first period.

The question of the archive remains the same: What comes first? Even better: Who comes first? And second?

At the end of the preceding chapter, the first *coup de théâtre* involving a "crucial episode" and a "canonical text": Yerushalmi had established the extraordinary archive we inscribed in the exergue. He had given his readers the unique copy given, but first of all returned, by the arch-patriarch to the patriarch, by Jakob to Sigmund, and yet, right on the substrate of its "new skin," the *figurative* reminder of a circumcision, the impression left on his body by the archive of a dissymmetrical covenant without contract, of a heteronomic covenant to which Sigmund Shelomoh subscribed before even knowing how to sign—much less countersign—his name. In the bottomless thickness of this inscription *en abyme,* in the instant of the archio-nomological event, under the new skin of a book that consigns the new skin, wounded and blessed, of a newborn, there resonated already the words intended for the newborn of a God speaking to him in him ("within you") even before he could speak, giving him to understand, to hear, in truth to read or to decipher: "Go, read my Book that I have written."

Giving us this archive to read, offering it to us in the course of a masterly decipherment, Yerushalmi, in turn, means less to *give* than to *give back.* He acts a bit like Jakob, who does not give Sigmund his Bible but rather gives it back to him. Returns it to him. In giving us this document to read, this true scholar wants also to give back to Freud his own competence, his own capacity to receive and thus to read the Hebrew inscription. He wants above all to make him confess it. Because Freud, and this is the declared aim of Yerushalmi's demonstration, must have known, from a young age, how to read the dedication. He ought, in consequence, to have confessed belonging, thus making his Hebrew culture public, or doing so more clearly than he did. Yerushalmi recalled all Freud's denials on this subject, concerning his own family or himself (all emancipated *Aufklärer!* he claimed, all Voltairians! and who retained little of Jewish culture!). Like Freud's father, the scholar seeks to call Sigmund Shelomoh back to the covenant by establishing, that is to say, by restoring, the covenant. The scholar repeats, in a way, the gesture of the father. He recalls or he repeats the circumcision, even if the one and the other can only do it, of course, *by figure.*

After the first, a second *coup de théâtre:* it is the moment when Professor Yerushalmi, with the incontestable authority of the scholar but in an apparently more filial position, addresses or rather pretends to address Professor Freud, in truth Freud's ghost, directly.

That the position then is more filial, that it manifests the love and the respect of a son, in no way contradicts the repetition of the paternal gesture. Quite possibly it confirms and relaunches it *en abyme*. A scholar addressing a phantom recalls irresistibly the opening of *Hamlet*. At the spectral apparition of the dead father, Marcellus implores Horatio: "Thou art a Scholler, speake to it, Horatio." I have tried to show elsewhere that though the classical scholar did not believe in phantoms and truly would not know how to speak to them, even forbidding himself to do so, it is quite possible that Marcellus had anticipated the coming of a *scholar of the future,* a scholar who, in the future and so as to conceive of the future, would dare to speak to the phantom. A scholar who would dare to admit that he knows how to speak *to* the phantom, even claiming that this not only neither contradicts nor limits his scholarship but will in truth have conditioned it, at the price of some still-inconceivable complication that may yet prove the other one, that is, the phantom, to be correct. And perhaps always the paternal phantom, that is, who is in a position to be correct, to be proven correct—and to have the last word.

"Dear and most highly esteemed Professor Freud": so begins this letter. An intensely filial and respectful letter, indeed, but all the more bitter, cutting, merciless in the reproach, one would say murderous in the quibbling, if the other were not dead, and thus infinitely inaccessible in his all-powerful vulnerability.

These thirty-odd pages are not only to be classed as fiction, which would already be a break with the language that has dominated up to this point in the book, that is, the discourse of scholarship, the discourse of a historian, of a philologist, of an expert on the history of Judaism, of a biblical scholar, as they say, claiming to speak in all objectivity while basing himself on ancient or new archives—and the wealth of these novelties has to do in particular with the fact that certain of these documents, until now hardly visible or inaccessible, secret or private, have been newly interpreted, newly translated, newly illuminated from historical or philological viewpoints.

No, this fiction has another originality, which sets the fictionality of the "Monologue" as if *en abyme:* the apostrophe is addressed to a dead person, to the historian's object become spectral subject, the virtual addressee or interlocutor of a sort of open letter. Another archive effect. In its very fiction, this apostrophe enriches the corpus it claims to treat but which it enlarges and of which, in fact, it is henceforth a part. At the end of a tight discussion with the phantom, according to the intersected rules of psychoanalysis and of the Talmud, "in the spirit of *le-didakh,*" the signatory of the book and of the letter ends by interrogating the specter of Freud.

We will come to this. For the moment, we say the "book" and the "letter" because if the letter is apparently a part of the book, if the "Monologue with Freud" resembles a last chapter of the book, one can also note two other structural singularities about its relationship to the book which, at least according to the editorial convention of its bibliographic archivization, contains it within itself. In the first place, this fictitious "Monologue" is heterogeneous to the book, in its status, in its project, in its form; it is thus by pure juridical fiction that such a fiction is, in effect, bound in the same book signed by the same author, and that it is classified under eight "scientific" rubrics (nonfictional: neither poetic nor novelistic nor literary) in the bibliographic catalogue whose classical categories are all found at the beginning of the work. In the second place, this postscript of sorts retrospectively determines what precedes it. It does it in a decisive fashion, marking it indeed with an essential indecision, namely the umbilical opening of the future, which makes the words "Jew" and "science" indeterminate at the very least—or in any case accedes to their indetermination. Thus one can just as well say that the entire book is in advance contained, as if carried away, drawn in, engulfed by the abysmal element of the "Monologue," for which it constitutes a kind of long preface, an exergue, a preamble, or a foreword. The true title of the book, its most appropriate title, its truth, would indeed be *Monologue with Freud.* Let us note this at least on account of the archive: to recall that there could be no archiving without titles (hence without names and without the archontic principle of legitimization, without laws, without criteria of classification and of hierarchization, without order and without order, in the double sense of the word). In the course of this tête-à-tête discussion, but in the presence of the reader that *we* are (or God knows who) as *terstis,* third party or witness, Freud is no longer treated as a third person represented by his written works (public and private writings, clinical, theoretical, or autobiographical, institutional or not, psychoanalytic and political, scientific or "novelistic"—because Yerushalmi's entire book turns around a book by Freud that he himself wanted to present as a *fiction, Der Mann Moses, ein historischer Roman,* while aiming at a new concept of truth, that is, under the name of "historical truth," a truth that scholarship, historiography, and perhaps philosophy have some difficulty thinking through). Freud is thus no longer treated as a witness in the third person (*terstis*); he finds himself *called to witness* as a second person. A gesture incompatible in principle with the norms of classical scientific discourse, in particular with those of history or of philology, which had presided over the same book up to this point. In addition, the signatory of this monological letter all of a sudden proposes to this second person, who is at first addressed as "you" and not "he," to speak in terms of "we." And as he recognizes that this other does not have a true right of reply, he responds for him: "In what is at issue here, indeed has been so all along, we both have, as Jews, an equal stake. Therefore in speaking of the Jews I shall not say 'they.' I shall say 'we.' The distinction is familiar to you" [81].

By definition, because he is dead and thus incapable of responding, Freud can only acquiesce. He cannot refuse this community at once proposed and imposed. He can only say "yes" to this covenant into which he must enter *one more time.* Because he will have had to enter it, already, seven or eight days after his birth. *Mutatis mutandis,* this is the situation of absolute dissymmetry and heteronomy in which a son finds himself on being circumcised after the seventh day and on being made to enter into a covenant at a moment when it is out of the question that he respond, sign, or countersign. Here again, the archive marked once in his body, Freud hears himself recalled to the indestructible covenant that this extraordinary performative engages—*"I shall say 'we'"*—when it is addressed to a phantom or a newborn.

(Let us note at least in parentheses: the violence of this *communal* dissymmetry remains at once extraordinary and, precisely, most *common.* It is the origin of the *common,* happening each time we address someone, each time we call them while *supposing,* that is to say while *imposing* a "we," and thus while inscribing the other person into this situation of an at once spectral and patriarchic nursling.)

Everything happens here as if Yerushalmi had decided in turn to circumcise Freud, as if he felt an obligation yet to come ("I shall say 'we'") to recircumcise him by figure while confirming the covenant, as if he felt the duty, in truth, to repeat Jakob Freud's gesture when, in an inscription at once outside and inside the book, *right on* the Book, in *melitzah,* he reminded Shelomoh, "In the seventh in the days of the years of your life the Spirit of the Lord began to move you and spoke within you: Go, read in my Book that I have written . . . " [71].

(The memory without memory of a mark returns everywhere, about which we ought to debate with Freud, concerning his many rapid statements on this subject: it is clearly the question of the singluar archive named "circumcision." Although he speaks of it here and there from Freud's or from Jones's point of view, Yerushalmi does not place this mark, at least in its literalness, at the center of his book [6]—and the enigma of circumcision, notably in the great war between Judaism and Christianity, is quite often that of its literalness and of all that depends on this. Although I believe this question to be irreducible, in particular in the rereading of Freud, irreducible notably to that of castration, I must put it aside here, not without some regret, along with that of the phylacteries, those archives of skin or parchment covered with writing that Jewish men, here too, and not Jewish women, carry close to their body, on their arm and on their forehead: *right on the body* [*à même le corps*], like the sign of circumcision, but with a *being-right-on* [*être-à-même*] that this time does not exlude the detachment and the untying of the ligament, of the substrate, and of the text simultaneously.

In this deliberately filial scene that Yerushalmi has with the patriarch of psychoanalysis, the apostrophe is launched from the po-

---

6. The theme of circumcision is, however, taken up from several points of view in *Moses.* From a historical point of view, it is a "conducting fossil" (*Leit-fossil*) for investigating memory and interpreting the Israelites' relations with the servitude in and the exodus from Egypt (where circumcision was an indigenous practice). From a more structural point of view, circumcision is the symbolic substitute of the castration of the son by the primitive father.

sition of the father, the father of the dead father. The other speaks. It is often thus in scenes the son has with the father. Speech comes back to the grandfather. Speech *returns,* in French *la parole revient:* as act of speaking and as right to speech. Why is this monologue clearly not a monologue or a soliloquy? Because it plays on the irony of presenting itself as a "Monologue with . . . "? Because more than one person speaks? Undoubtedly, but there is more than the number. There is the order. For if the signatory of the monologue is not alone in signing, far from it, he is above all the *first* to do so. He speaks *from* the position of the other: he carries in himself, this mouthpiece, he bears the voice that could be that of Jakob Freud, namely the arch-patriarch of psychoanalysis. And thus, in the name of Jakob, the voice of all the arch-patriarchs in history, in Jewish history in particular, for example those who not only inscribe their sons in the covenant at the moment of circumcision, and do it more than once, literally or by figure, but do not cease to be surprised and to remain skeptical about the possibility that a daughter could speak in her own name.

I have just alluded to the last request that the signatory of this monologue without response addresses to Freud's phantom. This request is carried in a question; we must distinguish between the one and the other here; the request questions on the subject of Anna Freud: "your Antigone," says Yerushalmi in passing, Yerushalmi, who, clearly thus identifying Freud, his specter, with Oedipus, thinks perhaps—*perhaps*—that this will suffice to de-oedipalize his own relationship with Freud, as if there were no possibility of ever becoming Oedipus's Oedipus. In 1977, Anna Freud was invited by the Hebrew University of Jerusalem to inaugurate an endowed chair carrying the name of her—long dead—father. Unable to go—she too—she sends, she too, a written statement. In this other archive document, which Yerushalmi invests with passion, Anna declares, among other things, that the accusation according to which psychoanalysis is a "Jewish science," "under present circumstances, can serve as a title of honour" [100].

Yerushalmi asks himself whether this sentence *written* by Anna is indeed *signed* by Anna. Asking himself this, he asks his spectral interlocutor (he asks himself (of) his specter who would first have asked himself this) if his daughter spoke in her own name: as if he doubted that a daughter, above all the daughter of Freud, could speak in her own name, almost thirty years after the father's death, and above all as if he wished, still secretly (a secret which he says he wants to keep, that is to say, to share with Freud, to be alone in sharing with Freud), that she had always spoken in the name of her father, in the name of the father:

> In fact, I will limit myself even further and be content if you answer only one question: When your daughter conveyed those words to the congress in Jerusalem, *was she speaking in your name?*
> Please tell me, Professor. I promise I won't reveal your answer to anyone. [100]

These are the last words of the book. Everything seems to be sealed by this ultimate signature in the form of a promise. Secretly but visibly, sheltered by a secret he wants manifest, by a secret he is anxious to make public, Yerushalmi wishes that Anna-Antigone had only been the living spokesperson, the faithful interpreter, the voice bearer come to support her dead father and to represent his word, his name, his belonging, his thesis, and even his faith. What, according to Yerushalmi, did she say, then? That in spite of all Freud's strategic denials [*dénégations*], in spite of all the political precautions he expressed throughout his life concerning the universal (non-Jewish) essence of psychoanalysis, it ought to honor itself for being Jewish, for being a fundamentally, essentially, radically Jewish science, Jewish in a differnt sense from the anti-Semitic allegation, while revealing the "historical truth" of anti-Semitism.

It seems to me that Yerushalmi's thesis advances here while withdrawing itself. But it is a thesis with a rather particular status—and a paradoxical movement: it posits not so much what *is* as what *will have been* and *ought to* or *should be in the future,* namely that psychoanalysis should in the future have been a Jewish science (I will return in a moment to this temporal modality), in a sense, admittedly, which is radically different from that of the anti-Semitic denunciation, but which would bring to light, one more time, and according to a very Freudian gesture in its style and tradition, the truth that could be carried by the anti-Semitic unconscious.

We will return to this question in another form momentarily. For the time being, I will pull from this web a single interpretative thread, the one that concerns the archive. What happens to the status of the archive in this situation? Well, the day when in an absolutely exceptional, unprecedented, unique, and inaugural fashion, indeed one that is incompatible with the tradition and the very idea of science, of *ēpistēmē,* of *historia,* or of *theoria,* indeed of philosophy in the West, the day, and from the moment when a science presenting itself as such and under this name binds itself intrinsically not only to the history of a proper name, of a filiation, and of a house, here Freud's house, but to the name and to the law of a nation, of a people, or of a religion, here psychoanalysis as Jewish science, this would have the consequence, among others, of radically transforming the relationship of such a science to its own archive. And in the same stroke, having kept an essential account of the singularity of an *arkheion,* this would transform the concept of science and the concept of the archive. In the *classical* structure of their concept, a science, a philosophy, a theory, a theorem are or should be *intrinsically* independent of the singular archive of their history. We know well that these things (science, philosophy, theory, etc.) have a history, a rich and complex history that carries them and produces them in a thousand ways. We know well that in diverse and complicated ways, proper names and signatures count. But the structure of the theoretical, philosophical, scientific statement, and even when it concerns history, does not have, should not in principle have, an intrinsic and essential need for the archive, and for what binds the archive in all its forms to some proper name or to some body proper, to some (familial or national) filiation, to covenants, to secrets. It has no such need, in any case, in its relationship or in its claim to truth—in the classical sense of the term. But as soon as one speaks of a Jewish science, whatever one's | 45 understanding of this word (and I will come back to this in an instant), the archive becomes a founding moment for science as such: not only the history and the memory of singular events, of exemplary proper names, languages and filiations, but the deposition in an *arkheion* (which can be an ark or a temple), the consignation in a place of relative exteriority, whether it has to do with writings, documents, or ritualized marks on the body proper (for example, phylacteries or circumcision). At issue here is nothing less than taking seriously the question whether a science can depend on something like a circumcision. We are deliberately saying "something like a circumcision" to designate the place of this problem, a place that is itself problematic, between the figure and literalness. Can one be satisfied with Freud's many statements on circimcision, always quickly tied to castration or to the threat of castration? To explain the genesis of anti-Semitism, namely, the jealousy with regard to a people which presented itself, he says, as the favored eldest son of God, Freud evokes in his *Moses* the circumscribed isolation of the Jews, the isolation that cuts them off from the world, the solitude of their exclusion by a circumcision which, according to him, always recalls dreaded castration. This seems less interesting, in any case here, or less convincing, than the manner in which Freud characterizes the *impression* which circumcision leaves on those who are uncircumcised: "a disagreeable, uncanny [*unheimlich*] impression"[7] [*SE* 23:91]. (I have attempted elsewhere to show, and cannot go into it here, that each time the word *unheimlich* appears in Freud's text—and not only in the essay of this title, *Das Unheimlich*—one can localize an uncontrollable undecidability in the axiomatics, the epistemology, the logic, the order of the discourse and of the thetic or theoretic statements; and the same is true, in just as significant a way, of Heidegger.)

Yerushalmi undoubtedly thinks, and his book seems in any case to aim at demonstrating, that psychoanalysis is a Jewish science. It seems to aim for it in an original sense. Proposing a rigorous and "scientific" renewal of reading, he bases himself on an archive sometimes archaic (the oldest biblical or talmudic tradition), sometimes recently published. In any case he leaves his own demonstration suspended at the point where it might seem to be conclusive. The fundamental question remains without response. Without response on Freud's part. Yerushalmi clearly wants this to come from *Freud's mouth*. Freud must also say, in his own name, that he avows and proclaims, in an irreducible performative, that psychoanalysis should honor itself for being a Jewish science. A performative by

---

7. "Ferner hat unter den Sitten, durch die sich die Juden absonderten, die der Beschneidung einen unliebsamen, unheimlichen Eindruck gemacht."

which he would as much determine science, psychoanalytic science, as the essence of Jewishness, if not Judaism.

It goes without saying, if one could put it this way, that Freud's phantom does not respond. That is at least how things appear. But can this be trusted? In promising secrecy for a virtual response which keeps us waiting, which will always keep us waiting, the signatory of this monologue lets it be understood that Freud would never say in public, for example in a book and in what is destined to become public archive, what he thinks in truth secretly, like the monologuist who says "we," namely, that, yes, psychoanalysis is indeed a Jewish science. Is this not incidentally what he has *already*, in private, so often suggested? Is this not what he has *already* murmured in remarks, entrusted to letters, consigned in a thousand signs that Yerushalmi has inventoried, classed, put in order, interpreted with unprecedented vigilance and jubilation? But at the end of the book, the monologuist who says "we" says he is ready to respect the secret, to keep for his personal archives the response that the phantom, with its own mouth, could murmur in his ear in private.

Nothing seems to me more serious than what is in play in this conclusion, in the very secret of its opening, in the fiction of its suspense. For a large number of reasons. Some of them seem to be turned toward the past, others toward the future of the archive.

A. Concerning the former, those which look toward the past, I will say only a word. It will go in the direction of what, in Freud's eyes, and in particular in *The Rat Man,* ties the progress of science and of reason to the advent of the patriarchate. In a note which I do not have the time to read here and will comment on elsewhere, Freud makes three mistakes, with Lichtenberg, whose support he seeks. He makes a mistake in affirming that there can be no doubt about the identity of the mother, insofar as it depends on the witness of the senses, while the identity of the father always remains doubtful since it depends, and it alone, on a rational inference, as that "legal fiction" of which Stephen speaks in Joyce's *Ulysses.* However, better than ever today, if only with the possibility of surrogate mothers, prosthetic maternities, sperm banks, and all the artificial inseminations, as they are secured for us already and will be secured still more for us in the future by bio-genetic techno-science, we know that maternity is as inferred, constructed, and interpreted as paternity. And as paternal law. In truth, it has always been thus, for the one and for the other. Freud makes a second mistake in believing with Lichtenberg that paternity, *and it alone,* is as uncertain as the question of whether the moon is inhabited: we know today, in all objective certainty, that the moon is uninhabited, and, conversely, it is easier to see and to touch that satellite's soil than the certain identity of a mother. He makes a third mistake in drawing from all these errors, illusions, or phantasms a phallogocentric conclusion: because of this presumed call to reason in the assignation of paternity, beyond the "witness of the senses," the passage to patriarchy marked the civilizing triumph of reason over sensibility, of science over perception.

In doubting that Anna-Antigone had spoken, from London to Jerusalem, in her own name, in visibly hoping that she had spoken in the name of the father—of her dead father—what does the signatory of the "Monologue with Freud" aim to overprint in the "we" of this unilateral contract and of this covenant, in this recircumcision of Freud? Well, he perhaps inscribes, perhaps (I am indeed saying *perhaps*), as if he were signing his name, a discreet but energetic and ineffaceable virility: *we* the fathers, we the archons, we the patriarchs, guardians of the archive and of the law. I say *perhaps,* because all these questions remain as suspended as the future to which I now turn.

I am indeed saying "perhaps," as Yerushalmi says "perhaps" at one of the most decisive moments of his suspended conclusions ("Absurd? Possibly. But *tomer dokh*—perhaps, after all . . . ?" [99]). What is at issue here is coming to a conclusion on the subject of Freud's secret, of his dissimulated or unavowable thought according to which psychoanalysis would be a Judaism without God; or according to which, concerning the future of Laius and of Oedipus or the future of religion, there would be no hope. "[Y]ou may very well be right," says Yerushalmi, who sees in the closure of the future, in hopelessness, in the nonpromise, more than in the atheism, what is least Jewish, most un-Jewish, in Freud; such that Jewishness here, if not Judaism, comes down, in its minimal essence, but as science itself, to the openness of the future. "But it is on this question of hope or hopelessness," Yerushalmi will say to Freud, "even more than on God or godlessness, that your teaching may be at its most un-Jewish" [95].[8] I stress this essential modality of the *perhaps*, as I am always tempted to do. It seems to me to be irreducible. Nietzsche claimed to recognize the thinkers of the future by their courage to say *perhaps*. I emphasize "perhaps" for yet another reason, while alluding to that patriarchal filiation of elders into which Yerushalmi seems to inscribe himself, at least by one of his gestures. Because he also asks Professor Freud a remarkable question about the identity of the mother, in his oedipal schema, perhaps a nonsensible identity, shielded perhaps from the witness of the senses, like the "legal fiction" of the father and even more than this because this time the woman would be the law itself:

> the Torah, the Teaching, the revelation, the Torah which in Hebrew is grammatically feminine and which is midrashically compared to a bride. It is over possession of her that Christianity, the younger son, came to challenge, not so much the Father as Judaism, the elder son. For this struggle "sibling rivalry" is perhaps too tame a phrase. Psychologically (and alas, all too often even historically) we are talking about fratricide. [92][9]

B.   Yes, let us rather speak of the future. Just before asking his question of the phantom of the patriarch, of the archontic specter of psychoanalysis, at the moment he promises to keep the secret, above all if he confirms that psychoanalysis is indeed a Jewish science, Yerushalmi takes the risk of making a decisive gesture. In a

8. Yerushalmi indeed distinguishes, and we will come back to this later, between Jewishness and Judaism. Judaism can be "terminable" and finite, as religion, tradition, or culture; Jewishness is not. One cannot translate "at its most un-Jewish" by "the furthest away from Judaism [*la plus éloignée du juda-ïsme*]," as the French translation does, without the risk of betraying or missing the very thesis of this book.

9. On this question of the brother, between Judaism and Christianity and in particular in the institution of psychoanalysis, permit me to refer you to *Politiques de l'amitié*, notably 310 ff. Devoting some fine pages to this question of fratricide, Yerushalmi puts forth the hypothesis according to which the figure of Cain offers an explanation which is "as potent" as that of Oedipus.

stroke, in a single paragraph, he overturns the entire epistemological axiomatic which had seemed up to this point to be a presupposition of his discourse. To describe this gesture I will select, once again, only what concerns the archive. First of all, it seems that in private, and I stress this point, in a *private letter,* Freud had already given, in the essentials, the very response that Yerushalmi seems to be waiting for or pretends to be waiting for, by promising to keep it to himself, as if he wanted to have for himself in secret, here, for his very own self, Josef Hayim Yerushalmi, the principle of an equally private response which Freud had *already* given (sixty-five years earlier!) to Enrico Morselli. As if he wanted to share with Freud, all alone, a secret that Freud had already confided to someone else, before Yerushalmi was even born: "In 1926," Yerushalmi writes, "you wrote privately to Enrico Morselli that you were not sure that his notion that psychoanalysis is a direct product of the Jewish mind is correct, but that if it is, you 'wouldn't be ashamed'" [100].

After having cited this private document, Yerushalmi adds a remark. It displaces in one stroke the whole question of the equation between Judaism and psychoanalysis. The two terms of such an equation become equally unknown, indeterminate, yet to be determined, totally given over to the future. Let us read this declaration, on the last page of the "Monologue":

> Professor Freud, at this point I find it futile to ask whether, genetically or structurally, psychoanalysis is really a Jewish science; that we shall know, if it is at all knowable, only when much future work has been done. Much will depend, of course, on how the very terms *Jewish* and *science* are to be defined. Right now, leaving the semantic and epistemological questions aside, I want only to know whether *you* ultimately came to believe it to be so. [100]

Yerushalmi emphasizes *you:* what is important is not so much the content of what Freud would say—Freud, moreover, has already acknowledged it in a way—as the fact that he should say it, *him* ("you"), with his mouth, and sign it henceforth with his name, and sign it as one subscribes to a belief: "whether *you* ultimately came to believe it to be so." This is *only* what he *wants to know:* "I want only to know whether *you* ultimately came to believe it to be so." Time and age count. Yerushalmi knows, and he was the first to recall it, that Freud *believed* this, at least sixty-five years earlier. If he asks it of him again, if he asks for more, if he seems to ask a new confirmation of him, it is as if he wanted the last word, the last will, the ultimate signature ("ultimately") of a dying father— and to be even more sure, of an already dead father. He wants an ultimate repetition, at the last minute; he asks for an eneffaceable countersignature, of what Freud said sixty-five years earlier and on quite a few other occasions. This last engagement ought to be ir-reversible, by definition. Engaging a dead person, it would no longer be subject to the strategic calculations, to the denials of the living Freud, and to the retractions of the founder of a psycho-analysis exposed to all the anti-Semitic violences.

This declaration seems to change all the signs. It is this, this alone, it seems to me, that can carry and justify the book's subtitle, *Judaism Terminable and Interminable.* It leaves open to the future, not only the definition, hence the determinability as much as the terminability, of Judaism, but also those of psychoanalysis. Up to this point, in any case up to the opening of this fictive monologue, Yerushalmi had measured his discourse—for the bulk of what, in theory, was shown and demonstrated—on the classical norms of knowledge, of scholarship, and of epistemology which dominate in every scientific community: here, the objectivity of the historian, of the archivist, of the sociologist, of the philologist, the reference to stable themes and concepts, the relative exteriority in relation to the object, particularly in relation to an archive determined as *already given, in the past* or in any case only *incomplete,* determinable and thus terminable in a future itself determinable as future present, domination of the constative over the performative, etc. This is how one can interpret the remark, made "in passing," concerning the discovery and the unexpected publication, in 1980, of the private archive of Sabina Spielrein. "This discovery," Yerushalmi notes, "should also serve to remind us of how incomplete and tentative any conclusions must be in our reconstructions of the history of psychoanalysis, until the mounds of materials still unpublished or deliberately restricted are made available" [44]. An incompleteness of the archive, and thus a certain determinability of the future, should be taken into consideration by the historian in any "reconstructions of the history of psychoanalysis." Now this incompleteness is of an entirely different order from that of the future which is in question at the end of the "Monologue." In the middle of the book, what was in question was still an incompleteness and a future that belong to the normal time of scientific progress. Without a doubt, at the end of the "Monologue" Yerushalmi again alludes to the future of some "future work." But the future of which he then speaks, and above all when it concerns the concepts of science and of Jewishness, is not of the order of such a relative incompleteness. It is no longer only the provisional indetermination that opens the ordinary field of a scientific work in progress and always unfinished, in particular because new archives can still be discovered, come out of secrecy or the private sphere, so as to undergo new interpretations. It is no longer a question of the same time, of the same field, and of the same relationship to the archive. At the moment when the historian declares to the patriarch that it would be "futile to ask whether, genetically or structurally, psychoanalysis is really a Jewish science," and when he adds: "that we shall know, *if it is at all knowable* [my emphasis], only when much future work has been done. Much will depend, of course, on how the very terms *Jewish* and *science* are to be defined," at this moment he changes registers and times entirely. In a stroke, he suspends all the axiomatic assurances, norms, and rules which had served him until now in organizing the scientific work, notably historiographic criticism, and in particular its relationship to the known and unknown archive. The very order of knowledge, at least of classical knowledge, is suspended. At issue is another concept of the future, to which we will return.

Since the questions that dominate the whole book, up to this "Monologue," concern the relations between Judaism and science, notably that science which psychoanalysis has wanted to be, Yerushalmi the scholar presumed continuously the knowledge of what "science" and "Judaism" meant. When an evaluation of the scientific character of psychoanalysis was in question, the historian often showed himself to be very severe and without appeal, concerning what he calls, in this book as in *Zakhor: Jewish History and Jewish Memory,* Freud's Lamarckism or "psycho-Lamarckism" [109]:[10] it is an antiquity condemned by the state of science, of a science which is not Yerushalmi's science and of which he invokes the results, in sum, from the exterior, as would a historian, who would content himself to record the results that are validated, at a particular moment, by a scientific community in which he does not actively participate and of which he does not share the competencies. On the other hand, Yerushalmi accepts, we can suppose, that he belongs to the scientific community of historians or of sociologists of culture, in particular of Jewish culture (he is professor of "Jewish History, Culture, and Society"). He shares actively and brilliantly in its productions, he increases and refines its abilities. But in what has to do with the genetics or the history of life, he accepts the role of neutral observer and in the end of doxographer. He must know that in this domain things are more turbulent and more open to the future than ever, more than anywhere else, and not without some relation to the future status of archivization. The epistemological status that he claims for his discourse would thus merit a thorough study. We shall only set up the cartography of the borders he assigns himself. This is not so easy, given the mobility of such limits. It seems that in the quasi-totality of the work, and up to the threshold of the "Monologue," the author presents himself as a historian who claims to hold himself deliberately exterior to his object. The historian, the subject of this historical knowledge, does not then present himself either as a Jew or as a psychoanalyst, as such. He treats the psychoanalytic archive as data, the right of access to which, the intelligibility, the evaluation of which are not properly the affair either of the Jew or of the psychoanalyst. On many occasions, Yerushalmi claims this distance as the very condition for the history he intends to write. He does it, for example, by putting these words of Philippe Ariès in the exergue of his last chapter, just before the "Monologue"—words that for

10. In a *postscript* of 1987 which does not appear in the first edition.

my part (and as is often the case for what Ariès says and does in general) I find more than problematic:

> One can make an attempt at the history of behavior, that is to say, at a psychological history, without being oneself either a psychologist or a psychoanalyst and while keeping oneself at a distance from the theories, the vocabulary and even the methods of modern psychology, and nevertheless to engage these very psychologists on their terrain. If one is born a historian one becomes a psychologist in one's own fashion. [57]

To express briefly my perplexity on this point, and why I do not share Yerushalmi's confidence when he cites such a remark, finding in it some backing no doubt, I wonder what it could mean to be "born a historian" ("Si on naît historien . . . ") and to base one's authority on this from an epistemological point of view. And above all, *concesso non dato,* supposing that, in such conditions, one could do a psychological history, this would not suffice to do a history of psychology, even less of psychoanalysis; and above all not at this point where this science, this *project* for a science at least, which is called psychoanalysis, claims to transform the very status of the historian's object, the structure of the archive, the concept of "historical truth," indeed of science in general, the methods of deciphering the archive, the implication of the subject in the space he claims to objectivize, and notably the topology of all the internal/external partitions that structure this subject and make of him a place for archives in relation to which no objectivization is pure, nor in truth rigorously possible, which is to say, complete and terminable. Even a classical historian of science should know from the inside the content of the sciences of which he does the history. And if this content concerns in fact historiography, there is no good method or good epistemology for authorizing oneself to put it into parentheses. One deprives oneself in this case of the elementary conditions, of the minimal semantic stability, and almost of the grammar which would allow one to speak about that of which one speaks. To want to speak about psychoanalysis, to claim to do the history of psychoanalysis from a purely apsychoanalytic point of view, purified of all psychoanalysis, to the point of believing one could erase the traces of any Freudian impression, is like claiming the right to speak without knowing what one's speaking about, without even wanting to hear anything about it. This structure is not only valid for the history of psychoanalysis, or for any discourse on psychoanalysis, it is valid at least for all the so-called social or human sciences, but it receives a singular inflection here which we must examine a bit more closely.

In fact, Yerushalmi knows that he cannot have this exteriority. He knows it too well. To liberate his discourse of all Freudian preimpression is not only impossible, it would be illegitimate. But as he also doesn't want to renounce this alleged constative and theoretical neutrality which the classical scholar or historian claims as his norm, the position of his discourse here, in any case in the better part of his book and before the "Monologue," is double, equivocal, unstable, I would even say exquisitely tormented. Doomed to denial, sometimes avowed in its very denial. At once persecuted and translated by the symptoms that call irresistibly for a postscript, namely, this "Monologue with Freud," which resembles—or pretends to resemble—the beginning of an analysis and the declared confession of a transfer. Whether it resembles or pretends to resemble, this postscript undoubtedly carries, in truth, in its very fiction, the truth of the book. This is marked in particular in the trembling of a gesture and the instability of a status: the historian refuses to be a psychoanalyst but also refrains from *not* being a psychoanalyst.

We shall take only two examples, precisely where they affect a double relationship to the archive.

The first, the *arch-example,* shows us the desire of an admirable historian who wants in sum to be the first archivist, the first to discover the archive, the archaeologist and perhaps the archon of the archive. The first archivist institutes the archive as it should be, that is to say, not only in exhibiting the document but in *establishing* it. He reads it, interprets it, classes it. In this case, what is in play is all the more serious, as the document turns out to keep this inscription in the form of a dedication that accompanies a reiterated gift, the second present, the restitution of the Philippsohn Bible by the arch-patriarch to the patriarch of psychoanalysis, the present which Jakob son of R. Shelomoh Freid gives to Shelomoh Sigmund

Freud, thirty-five years after a circumcision, which it begins by re-calling to him in naming the Ark of the Covenant and the Tablets of the Law. Yerushalmi announces in sum that he will be the first (*after Freud*), indeed the only person (*after Freud*) to open, if not to hold, the archive of what he calls "one crucial episode." He would like, as we will see, to be the first here: the first *after Freud,* the first second, an eldest son, the first second and thus for a moment alone with Freud, alone in sharing a secret. (He is certainly not the only one or the first to want to be the first *after Freud* and thus alone with Freud; we have several others in France, in that French line-age from which Yerushalmi seems to want to shield himself—but why?—as from the plague.)

This being the case, for what reason does he still hesitate? Why is he so embarrassed about the question as to whether he proceeds in the manner of those whom he will later call "ordinary histori-ans" [86], or already in the manner of a psychoanalyst historian, in other words, in some sense, in the manner of an inheritor in the lineage of the patriarchs or arch-patriarchs whose archive he deci-phers for the first time, and "properly"? He says "properly" twice. And he claims to be *neither an analyst nor a non-analyst,* denying the two hypotheses at once, thus not denying either one, succes-sively or simultaneously. The passage is as follows:

> There is one crucial episode involving Jakob and Sigmund Freud which *has not yet been properly assessed* [my emphasis], not least because it involves a Hebrew text which has never been *properly transcribed* [again my emphasis] (the handwriting is ad-mittedly difficult), *let alone adequately glossed*[45] [my emphasis]. But it is, in effect, the one canonical text of Jakob Freud at our disposal. In what follows I neither presume to dignify my recon-struction as "psychoanalytic" (though it is no less so than others that pretend to be) [this will be a magnificent and luminous reading] nor, given the limitations of a single text, do I claim more than a partial insight. [70][11]

11. I recommend note 45 [133–34] to those who may be further interested in Yerushalmi's concern to mark at once the priority and the exclusive pro-

Here now is the *following* example, the example also of *that which follows,* a *second* example of primo-secondariness, the example of this eldest son, of this second eldest son of Jakob Freud, of this double status of a historian who refuses without wanting to refuse to be without being a psychoanalyst. Yerushalmi says to us in the conditonal tense what he would say, and thus what he says, if he were to permit himself what he thus permits himself, namely, "the luxury of a technical psychoanalytic term—an example of 'deferred obedience'": "should I finally allow myself the luxury of a technical psychoanalytic term—an example of 'deferred obedience'" [77]. At issue here is the deferred obedience of Freud to his father, of the patriarch to the arch-patriarch. (One has a hard time halting the sequence and the scene: in a few minutes, we will perhaps speak of Yerushalmi's "deferred obedience" to each of these figures—and draw from this some conclusions.)

A precious documentary question, once again, of archaeological excavation and of the detection of the archive. It concerns a single sentence in a sort of intellectual autobiography.[12] Freud added this sentence, as an expression of remorse, only in 1935, one year after the first sketch of *Moses.* It is important to know that this sentence was omitted, "accidentally," the *Standard Edition* says, in the *Gesammelte Werke* of 1948; and it is also absent, and for good reason, from the French translation of Marie Bonaparte, which dates from 1928. But this omission was maintained in later editions, at least until 1950. One could add this small philological remark to the file Freud himself investigates in chapter 6 of the second essay of his *Moses* [*SE* 23:41 ff.], in the course of those rich pages on archivization, the oral tradition and the written tradition, biblical exegesis, historiography, and all the *Entstellungen,* all the deformations of a text which he compares to murders. I now cite the sentence added by Freud in 1935, as it is cited by Yerushalmi:

priety of this reading, what is appropriate about it and what remains proper to it. This note concerns the competition of two other transcriptions, translations, and analyses.

12. The text, *Selbstdarstellungen,* first published in *Die Medizin der Gegenwart* (1925), appeared in English as *An Autobiographical Study* [*SE* 20:7–70].

My deep engrossment in the Bible story (almost as soon as I had learned the art of reading) had, as I recognized much later, an enduring effect upon the direction of my interest. [*SE* 20:8; qtd. in Yerushalmi 77]

Yerushalmi interprets the document which this addition constitutes, ten years after the first edition:

> Significantly, the last sentence did not appear in the first edition. It was added only in 1935, the year after the completion of the manuscript draft of *Moses*. Only now, in retrospect, did Freud realize the full impact of the study of the Bible on his life, and only now did he fully acknowledge it. In this sense *Moses and Monotheism* represents, at last, a fulfilment of Jakob Freud's mandate or—should I finally allow myself the luxury of a technical psychoanalytic term—an example of "deferred obedience." [77]

What should we think of this "deferred obedience"? (I will note first in parentheses that the little sentence on the "deep engrossment in the Bible" was immediately followed by another, which Yerushalmi does not cite. Judging it to be legitimately beyond the domain of his remarks, he cuts just before it. From the first edition on, this sentence declared the admiring and fascinated hope which Freud had very early for what "Darwin's theories"—he does not name Lamarck here—were able to promise at the time for the future of science.)

In this concept of "deferred obedience," one can be tempted to recognize one of the keys or, if you prefer, one of the seals of this *arkheion,* I mean of this book by Yerushalmi, at least as an archival book on the archive. In fact, the key or the seal, what signs and offers to be read is less a concept, the Freudian concept of "deferred obedience," than its implementation by Yerushalmi. This implementation takes the concept without taking it, uses it without using it: it "mentions" rather than "uses" it, as a *speech acts* theorist would say; it makes a concept (*Begriff*) out of it which in turn grasps without grasping, comprehends without taking. And this double gesture of someone who intends at once to assume and not to assume the theoretico-scientific responsibility of such a concept, this is precisely the scene of "luxury" which the conditional coquetry describes: "should I finally allow myself the luxury of a technical psychoanalytic term—an example of 'deferred obedience.'" The play of this luxury is at the joint between truth and fiction. It assures the unity of the book, it seems to me, insofar as it articulates together four chapters of "scholarship" which see themselves as conforming to the traditional norms of scientificity, and a last chapter of fictive monologue—with a specter who, at least apparently, no longer responds. But the last chapter, the most fictive, is certainly not the least true. In its own way, even if it does not say the truth, it *makes* the truth, in the sense in which Augustine could say this of confession. It inspires something else in us about the truth of the truth: about the history of the truth, as about the truth of the enigmatic difference Freud wanted to mark between "material truth" and "historical truth." I cannot imagine a better introduction to the question of the archive, today, than the very stakes of this vertiginous difference.

How does the "luxury" of this "deferred obedience" join, according to me, the two periods of this book? The history of this concept (*nachträgliche Gehorsam,* "docility after the fact"), as Yerushalmi retraces it in a few lines, goes back to *Totem and Taboo.*[13] Freud notes there that "The dead father became stronger than the living one. . . . in accordance with the psychological procedure so familiar to us in psycho-analyses under the name of 'deferred obedience'" [*SE* 13:143].

From this very convincing staging, Yerushalmi draws all the consequences. Coming from *Totem and Taboo,* the "technical" concept of "deferred obedience" is borrowed and transferred, here too with the required delay, onto Freud himself, Freud the author of *Moses.* The deferred docility here becomes that of Sigmund to Jakob, his father:

13. It is a passage that I attempted to interpret previously, in its relationship to the origin of the law and with reference to Kafka's *Vor dem Gesetz.* Cf. "Préjugés: Devant la loi."

In writing *Moses and Monotheism* he belatedly obeys the father and fulfills his mandate by returning to the intensive study of the Bible, but at the same time he maintains his independence from his father through his interpretation. He rejects the "material truth" of the biblical narrative but rejoices in his discovery of its "historical truth." [78]

"Where does this leave us?" Yerushalmi asks before praising Lou Andreas-Salomé, who says she read a new form of the "return of the repressed" in *Moses,* this time not in the form of "phantoms out of the past" but rather in the form of what one could call a "triumph of life." The afterlife [*survivance*] no longer means death and the return of the specter, but the surviving of an excess of life which resists annihilation ("the survival of the most triumphant vital elements of the past") [78].

Two pages later, at the beginning of the "Monologue with Freud," Yerushalmi dares to address himself to Freud. Thus he himself speaks to one of these "phantoms out of the past." This new "scholar" seems to have come straight from *Hamlet:* "Thou art a Scholler; speake to it, Horatio." He apostrophizes the paternal specter of Professor Freud. This is an uncommon and perhaps unprecedented scene in the history of psychoanalysis. Though I would like to, I cannot do justice either to the veiled richness or to the bottomless irony of this extraordinary "Monologue," during which a historian has dared to cross a limit before which "ordinary historians" [86] have always been intimidated. I shall hold myself, once again, to the instance of the archive. And I shall undoubtedly teach nothing to the author of this great "Monologue with Freud" as I venture a few remarks which, obedient in turn, I will group under the title of "deferred obedience."

Which one? No longer (1) the obedience "after the fact" Freud speaks of in *Totem and Taboo,* no longer (2) the one Yerushalmi speaks of (that of Sigmund to Jakob, his father), but indeed (3) the deferred docility of Yerushalmi with respect to Freud.

Let us describe this time of repetition with the words Yerushalmi reserves for Freud:

1.   Yerushalmi in turn addresses himself at last and "belatedly" to Freud's phantom with filial respect.

2.   He returns in turn to the "intensive study of the Bible."

3.   He "maintains his independence." Mimicking a doubly fictitious parricide, he argues bitterly with a master whose psychoanalytic rules and premises he accepts. He also interiorizes the discourse of the patriarch, at least in respecting the "according to you" of the *le-didakh,* talmudic *terminus technicus.* All these signs remind us that Yerushalmi also "belatedly obeys the father," whether he wants to or not. He identifies with him while interiorizing him like a phantom who speaks in him before him. He offers him hospitality and goes so far as to confess to him not without fervor: "you are real and, for me, curiously present" [81].

Now let us not forget, this is also the phantom of an expert in phantoms. The expert had even stressed that what is most interesting in repression is what one does not manage to repress. The phantom thus makes the law—even, and more than ever, when one contests him. Like the father of Hamlet behind his visor, and by virtue of a *visor effect,* the specter sees without being seen. He thus reestablishes the heteronomy. He finds himself confirmed and repeated in the very protest one claims to oppose to him. He dictates even the words of the person who addresses him, for example the strange word "engrossment": after having used it to translate Freud's belated confession about his impregnation by biblical culture, Yerushalmi applies it now to himself, deliberately or not, to describe his own investment in this archive of Freud which has become a sort of Bible for him, a spectral Bible. He speaks of his "engrossment": by or in Freud's corpus. With a gesture in which it is impossible to discern between love and hate, but also between their simulacral doubles, Yerushalmi painfully, laboriously justifies himself to Freud, one would almost say in asking for his forgiveness. He even recalls, if one must believe him, that, unlike other inheritors and wayward sons, he has not looked for the secrets or the weaknesses of the master, of the one who remains, like Goethe, through the "autobiographical records, a careful concealer":

I have not rummaged through your life in search of flaws. Those uncovered by others in recent years have not affected my engrossment in your uncommon achievement, which continues to pursue me "like an unlaid ghost." [82]

Naturally, by all appearances, we believe we know that *the phantom does not respond*. He will never again respond, Yerushalmi knows it. On the strength of more than one reason, Freud will never again speak.

1. He will never again respond in the future because he had *already* responded, and even with what Yerushalmi wants to hear from his lips—to Morselli for example, more than half a century earlier.

2. He will never again respond because he will have been in a position to have, *already, always* responded.

3. He will never again respond because it is a phantom, thus a dead person.

4. He will never again respond because it is the phantom, of an analyst; and perhaps because the analyst should withdraw to this spectral position, the place of the dead person, from which, leaving one to speak, he makes one speak, never responding except to silence himself, only being silent to let the patient speak, long enough to transfer, to interpret, to work.

So here is what we *believe we know* at least, here is the appearance: the other will never again respond. Now in spite of these necessities, these obvious facts and these substantiated certitudes, in spite of all the reassuring assurances which such a knowing or such a believing-to-know despenses to us, through them, the phantom continues to speak. Perhaps he does not respond, but he speaks. A phantom speaks. What does this mean? In the first place or in a preliminary way, this means that without responding it disposes of a response, a bit like the answering machine whose voice outlives its moment of recording: you call, the other person is dead, now, whether you know it or not, and the voice responds to you, in a very precise fashion, sometimes cheerfully, it instructs you, it can even give you instructions, make declarations to you, address your requests, prayers, promises, injunctions. Supposing, *concesso non dato,* that a living being ever responds in an absolutely living and infinitely well-adjusted manner, without the least automatism, without ever having an archival technique overflow the singularity of an event, we know in any case that a spectral response (thus informed by a *technē* and inscribed in an archive) is always possible. There would be neither history nor tradition nor culture without that possibility. It is this that we are speaking of here. It is this, in truth, that we must answer for.

We cannot reconstitute here the *virtual* exchange of questions and answers set in motion in such a "Monologue" on the subject of the very *content* of *Moses*. This entire talmudico-psychoanalytic discussion is fascinating and passionate. But can one not then say that *a priori* it shows Freud to be right? Can one not claim that the very structure of this scene, the formal logic of the arguments, the topology and the strategy of the interlocutors (living or spectral) show Freud *to be right,* even and, perhaps, above all where he is wrong, from the point of view of "material truth"? Even where the dead person may be put to death again, Freud like so many others, from Laius to Moses? Even where he is accused of so many shortcomings by the one who proceeds while *repeating* "I repeat: I do not blame you" [98]?

"To do justice." Yet again, I would like to but cannot *do justice* to the intense and rich discussion staged by this final "Monologue." If I should fail to do it, which seems to me unfortunately inevitable, it is not due only to some limit or another (personal, factual, alas real), it is not due even to the lack of time. This fatal "injustice" is due to the necessity of *showing, a priori,* the person occupying the *position* of Freud here *to be right.* This is the strange violence I would like to speak of (also out of concern for justice, because I shall no doubt be unjust out of concern for justice) while making myself in turn guilty of it *a priori.*

Simultaneously fictive and effective, taut, dramatic, as generous as it is implacable, this "Monologue" does not deprive the other of his right to speak. Not without injustice can one say that Freud has no chance to speak. He is the first to speak, in a certain sense, and the last word is offered to him. The right to speak is *left, given* or *lent* to him. I would need hours to justify any one of these three words. What interests me here, in the first place, is the nearly *formal* fatality of a performative effect. | 63

(I shall have to limit myself to this formality, renouncing the detailed discussion of the content of the analyses. But before returning to this structural fatality, I would like to give an example, at least in parentheses and only as an indication, of what this discussion could be. At the beginning of the "Monologue with Freud," basing himself on certain citations of the Midrash, Yerushalmi proposes a first conclusion to "Professor Freud":

> If Moses had actually been killed by our forefathers, not only would the murder not have been repressed but—on the contrary—it would have been remembered and recorded [i.e., archived], eagerly and implacably, in the most vivid detail, the quintessential and ultimate exemplum of the sin of Israel's disobedience. [85]

This, in my opinion, is the sinews of the argument in this book. Now to affirm this, Yerushalmi must again suppose that the contradiction between the act of memory or of archivization on the one hand and repression on the other remains irreducible. As if one could not, precisely, recall and archive the very thing one represses, archive it while repressing it (because repression is an archivization), that is to say, to archive *otherwise,* to repress the archive while archiving the repression; *otherwise,* of course, and that is the whole problem, than according to the current, conscious, patent modes of archivization; *otherwise,* that is to say, according to the paths which have called to psychoanalytic deciphering, in truth to psychoanalysis itself. How can Yerushalmi be sure that the murder in question has not been abundantly recalled and archived ("remembered and recorded") in the memory of Israel? How can he claim to *prove* an absence of archive? How does one prove in general an absence of archive, if not in relying on classical norms (presence/absence of literal and explicit reference to this or to that, to a this or to a that which one supposes to be identical to themselves, and simply absent, *actually* absent, if they are not simply present, *actually* present; how can one not, and why not, take into account *unconscious,* and more generally *virtual* archives)? Now Yerushalmi knows very well that Freud's intention is to analyze, across the apparent absence of memory and of archive, all kinds of symptoms, signs, figures, metaphors, and metonymies that attest, at least virtually, an archival documentation where the "ordinary historian" identifies none. Whether one goes along with him or not in his demonstration, Freud claimed that the murder of Moses *effectively* left archives, documents, symptoms in the Jewish memory and even in the memory of humanity. Only the texts of this archive are not readable according to the paths of "ordinary history" and this is the very relevance of psychoanalysis, if it has one.

Let us go further, keeping close to the example chosen by Yerushalmi, who has the courage and the merit, the temerity even, to cite not only the Bible but "rabbis in the Midrash" who are still more "explicit" than the Bible in testifying *at least about an attempted murder*:

> And the entire community threatened to stone them with stones (Numbers 14:10). And who were they? Moses and Aaron. [But the verse continues] *when the glory of the Lord appeared [in the tent of meeting unto all the children of Israel]*. This teaches us that they [the Israelites] were throwing stones and the Cloud [of the Lord's Glory] would intercept them. [85]

Yerushalmi seems to conclude—and to want to convince Professor Freud—that if in fact they wanted to kill Moses (and Aaron), and if this intention has indeed remained in the memory and in the archive, what counts is that the Israelites did not "actually" kill him. This conclusion appears to be doubly fragile. And even from the Midrash point of view in question. First, without needing to convoke psychoanalysis yet, one should recognize that if the murder did not take place, if it remained virtual, if it only almost took place, *the intention to kill was effective, actual, and in truth accomplished*. There was acting out, the stones were thrown *in fact*, they continued to be thrown while only divine intervention intercepted them. The crime was not interrupted at any moment by Israelites themselves, going no further than their suspended intention, or renouncing in the face of the sin. There was thus not only *intention* but *attempt* to murder, *effective, actual* attempt, which only an exterior cause (a jurist would say an accident) diverted. Second, and this time taking into account a psychoanalytic logic, what difference is there between a murder and an intention to murder (above all if it is acted out, but even if it is not murder, even if the intention does not become attempt to murder)? Murder begins with the intention to kill. The unconscious does not know the difference here

| 65

between the virtual and the acutal, the intention and the action (a certain Judaism also, by the way), or at least does not model itself on the manner in which the conscious (as well as the law or the morals accorded to it) distributes the relations of the virtual, of the intentional, and of the actual. We will never have finished, we have not in truth begun, drawing all the ethico-juridical consequences from this. In any case, the unconscious may have kept the memory and the archive of the intention to kill, of the acting out of this desire to kill (as it is attested by the texts Yerushalmi himself cites, in particular this singular *Midrash*)—even if there has been repression; because a repression also archives that of which it dissimulates or encrypts the archives. What is more, we see well that the repression was not all that efficient: the will to kill, the acting out and the attempt to murder are avowed, they are literally inscribed in the archive. If Moses was not killed, it is only thanks to God. Left to themselves, the Israelites, who wanted to kill Moses, would have killed him: they did everything to kill him.

Earlier, Yerushalmi declared: "The vital question remains whether, if Moses had been murdered in the wilderness, *this* would have been forgotten or concealed" [84]. And everything in his text responds *no*. Now instead of signifying, as he believes he can claim, that if the murder did not leave any archives it is because it did not take place, it suffices to read the texts he himself cites to conclude the contrary: the intention to kill was effective, the acting out also, this left an archive, and even if there had not been acting out of the desire, the unconscious would have been able to keep the archive of the pure criminal intention, of its suspension or of its repression. We can say this, it would seem, without having to take sides (which I am not doing), but on the logical reading of the whole of this argumentation alone. And to extend the problematic field of an *archive of the virtual,* in its greatest generality, throughout and beyond psychoanalysis. The topology and the nomology we have analyzed up to now were able to necessitate, as an absolutely indispensable condition, the *full and effective actuality* of the taking-place, the reality, as they say, of the archived event. What will become of this when we will indeed have to remove the concept of virtuality from the couple that opposes it to actuality, to effectivity, or to reality? Will we be obliged to continue thinking that there is no thinkable archive for the virtual? For what happens in virtual space and time? It is hardly probable, this mutation is in progress, but it will be necessary, to keep a rigorous account of this other virtuality, to abandon or restructure from top to bottom our inherited concept of the archive. The moment has come to accept a great stirring in our conceptual archive, and in it to cross a "logic of the unconscious" with a way of thinking of the virtual which is no longer limited by the traditional philosophical opposition between act and power.)

Let us return now to what we called a moment ago the fatal and *formal* constraint of a performative effect. This effect is due to what the signatory of the "Monologue" *does,* in the scene he thinks he can organize, while playing or assuming a certain role in it. This effect seems to show the phantom to be right, in the very place where he could, perhaps, be wrong and lose in the conflict of arguments. Because the scene effectively repeats, and it could not be more obvious, everything Freud says both about the return of phantoms and, to use the words of Yerushalmi, about the "tense agon of Father and son" [95]. One could show this in detail. Such a repetition attests that "historical truth" which no breach of "material truth" will ever weaken. What confirms or demonstrates a certain truth of Freud's *Moses* is not Freud's book, or the arguments deployed there with more or less pertinence. It is not the contents of this "historical novel"; it is rather the scene of reading it provokes and in which the reader is inscribed in advance. For example in a fictive monologue which, in reading, contesting, or in calling to Freud, repeats in an exemplary fashion the logic of the event whose specter was described and whose structure was "performed" by the historical novel. The Freud of this *Freud's Moses* is indeed Yerushalmi's Moses. The strange result of this performative repetition, the irrepressible effectuation of this *enactment,* in any case what it unavoidably demonstrates, is that the interpretation of the archive (here, for example, Yerushalmi's book) can only illuminate, read, interpret, establish its object, namely a given inheritance, by inscribing itself into it, that is to say by opening it and by enriching it enough to have a rightful place in it. There is no meta-archive. Yerushalmi's book, including its fictive monologue, henceforth belongs to the corpus of Freud (and of Moses, etc.), whose name it also *carries*. The fact that this corpus and this name also remain spectral is perhaps a general structure of every archive. By incorporating the knowledge deployed in reference to it, the archive augments itself, engrosses itself, it gains in *auctoritas*. But in the same stroke it loses the absolute and meta-texual authority it might claim to have. One will never be able to objectivize it with no remainder. The archivist produces more archive, and that is why the archive is never closed. It opens out of the future.

How can we think about this fatal repetition, about repetition in general in its relationship to memory and the archive? It is easy to perceive, if not to interpret, the necessity of such a relationship, at least if one associates the archive, as naturally one is always tempted to do, with repetition, and repetition with the past. But it is the future that is at issue here, and the archive as an irreducible experience of the future.

And if there is a single trait about which Yerushalmi remains intractable, if there is an affirmation shielded from all discussion (psychoanalytic or talmudic), an unconditional affirmation, it is the affirmation of the future *to come* [*l'à-venir*] (in French, I prefer saying this with the to-come of the *avenir* rather than the *futur* so as to point toward the coming of an event rather than toward some future present).

The affirmation of the future *to come:* this is not a positive thesis. It is nothing other than the affirmation itself, the "yes," insofar as it is the condition of all promises or of all hope, of all awaiting, of all performativity, of all opening toward the future, whatever it may be, for science or for religion. I am prepared to subscribe without reserve to this reaffirmation made by Yerushalmi. With a speck of anxiety, in the back of my mind, a single speck of anxiety about a solitary point, which is not just any point. I will specify it with more precision in a moment. This unique point can be reduced, indeed, to the Unique, to the unity of the One and of the Unique.

The same affirmation of the future to come is repeated several times. It comes back at least according to three modalities, which also establish three places of opening. Let us give them the name of *doors.*

The three doors of the future to come resemble each other to the point of confusion, indeed, but they differ between themselves: at least in that they regularly turn on their hinges to open, one onto the other. Their topo-logic thus remains properly *disorienting*. One continually has the feeling of getting lost while retracing one's steps [*en revenant sur ses pas*]. What is a door doing when it opens onto a door? And above all onto a door one has *already* passed through, in the *passage* of what comes to pass, in the *passage* to come?

In naming these doors, I think or rather I dream of Walter Benjamin. In his *Theses on the Philosophy of History,* he designates the "narrow door" for the passage of the Messiah, "at each second." And he recalls also that "for the Jews the future to come nonetheless does not become a homogeneous and empty time" [1:2.702]. What could he have meant? Or, at least for the time being, what can we understand in this remark or make it say, this remark about the door of a future to come whose time would not be homogeneous?

Allow me thus to localize and identify what I call the three doors of the future to come, as I believe I can count them in the "Monologue with Freud."

The *last door* opens, of course, at the last sentence of the book. A remarkable and necessary location, decisive precisely where nothing is decided. It is not by chance that this last door takes the form of a promise, the promise of a secret kept secret. What happens when a historian promises to keep secret on the subject of an archive which is yet to be established? Who does this? Is he still a historian? To whom does he promise? Before whom? Before what law? Before what specter and before what witness does Yerushalmi pretend to commit himself for the future to keep Freud's response secret when he declares to him in the last words of the book: "Please tell me, Professor. I promise I won't reveal your answer to anyone."

How could the person who promises a secret to a specter still dare to say he is a historian? We would not believe him, even if he pretended to address the Professor as a colleague or a master. The historian speaks only of the past, Yerushalmi says this himself at the end of the first of his texts that I read, a text about the Marranos, with whom I have always secretly identified (but don't tell anyone) and whose crypto-Judaic history greatly resembles that of psychoanalysis after all. Regarding the "last Marranos," Yerushalmi writes:

> But are they really [the last]? History, as we have recently seen, is not always rational, it is rarely foreseeable. *The future, in spite of the appearances, always remains open. The historian's task, luckily, is to try to understand the past.* It is time for the historian to step aside to let the images speak. [Brenner and Yerushalmi 44, my emphasis]

At the date of this text on the Marranos (and Yerushalmi always dates twice at the moment of signing or archiving his works, according to two calendars, the Jewish one and the other one), what is at issue for him is letting the images speak in a book of photographs, that is, another species of archive. But each time a historian as such decides to "step aside and let . . . speak," for example to let a photographic specter or Freud's phantom in the monologue speak, it is the sign of a respect before the future to come of the future to come. Thus he is no longer a historian. Good sense tells us there is no history or archive of the future to come. A historian as such never looks to the future, which in the end does not concern him. But meaning something else altogether, is there a historian of the promise, a historian of the first door?

The *second door* leaves a double definition open to the future: both that of Jewishness and that of science. Definition open to a future radically *to come,* which is to say indeterminate, determined only by this opening of the future to come. Indetermination forcefully and doubly potentialized, indetermination *en abyme.*

In effect, *on the one hand,* it indetermines one indetermination by the other (Jewishness by science and science by Jewishness). I cite this essential passage a second time:

> Professor Freud, at this point I find it futile to ask whether, genetically or structurally, psychoanalysis is really a Jewish science; that we shall know, *if it is at all knowable* [my emphasis], only when much future work has been done. Much will depend,

70

of course, on how the very terms *Jewish* and *science* are to be defined.

This remark followed an allusion to "much future work" and it opened to infinity the gaping of the future in which the very possibility of knowledge remained conditional ("if it is at all knowable"). In other words, the definition of the two terms depends on the future. In this equation with two unknowns, only the future of science, in particular that of psychoanalysis, will say whether this science is Jewish, because it will tell us what science is and what Jewishness is. But only the future of Judaism (or rather of interminable Jewishness) will be able to guide and precede a science of Judaism (or rather of Jewishness), indeed a Jewish science. Now since the future of science can thus be correlative to Jewishness, there is every risk, or every chance, that in this logical aporia, the question is destined to remain without response; without response in any case in the form of theoretical knowledge or of *epistēmē*.

Hence, *on the other hand,* a second force of indetermination. It is readable in the several suspensive words that leave a possibility open: that this double question which binds Jewishness and science *does not come within the province of knowledge* and is heterogeneous to all theoretical statement: "that we shall know, *if it is at all knowable.*" Having arrived at these last lines of the book, we still cannot say anything pertinent about what binds science and Jewishness, about what stabilizes and guarantees these concepts (and thus those of the archives which are dependent on them). Nothing that seems scientifically relevant. I will say in passing that this is what neutralizes or perhaps invalidates all that Yerushalmi had wanted to demonstrate up to this point. This is what threatens it, at least in its theoretic value if not in its dramatic effect or its performative richness.

But there is something more serious and perhaps better: in the future, it is very possible that the solution to this equation with two unknowns will not come within the domain of theoretical knowledge, that is to say, of a declarative theorem. This is what is suggested by "if it is at all knowable." This epochal suspense gathers in an act all the energy of thought, an energy of virtuality, for once (*energeia* of a *dynamis*). The intensity of this suspension is vertiginous—and it gives vertigo while giving the only condition on which the future to come remains what it is: it is to come. The condition on which the future remains to come is not only that it not be known, but that it not be *knowable as such*. Its determination should no longer come under the order of knowledge or of a horizon of preknowledge but rather a coming or an event which one *allows* or *incites* to come (without *seeing* anything come) in an experience which is heterogeneous to all taking note, as to any horizon of waiting as such: that is to say, to all stabilizable theorems as such. It is a question of this performative to come whose archive no longer has any relation to the record of what is, to the record of the presence of what is or will have been *actually* present. I call this the *messianic*, and I distinguish it radically from all messianism.

The *third door* is also the first, and we have already passed through it. A few pages earlier, Yerushalmi had deployed the question of the future or the immortality of Oedipus. And what he had held in opposition to Freud, finally, is an experience of the future or of hopefulness which seems to him to be at once irreducible to oedipal repetition and irreducibly, *uniquely, exclusively Jewish, proper* to "Jewishness" if not to "Judaism." The subtitle of his book says "Judaism Terminable and Interminable." But Yerushalmi clearly marks that if Judaism is terminable, Jewishness is interminable [90]. It can survive Judaism. It can survive it as a heritage, which is to say, in a sense, *not without archive*, even if this archive should remain without substrate and without actuality. For Yerushalmi, there is indeed a determining and irreducible essence of Jewishness; it is already given and does not await the future. And this essence of Jewishness should not be mistaken as merging with Judaism, or with religion, or even with the belief in God. Now the Jewishness that does not await the future is precisely the waiting for the future, the opening of a relation to the future, the experience of the future. This is what would be proper to the "Jew" and to him alone: not only hope, not only a "hope for the future," but "the anticipation of a specific hope for the future" [95].

And this is where, in the name of the opening to the future, the discussion with Freud seems to be closed, even while in the last lines of the book it is the word "Jewish" (which can be the adjective for Jewishness as well as for Judaism) that Yerushalmi says remains to be defined in the future. Here is one of the passages that are most important to us on this subject. I shall emphasize certain phrases:

> Indeed, the charm of it all is that Oedipus is far from alien to the Bible itself, where the entire relationship between God and Man and especially between God and Israel is always the tense agon of Father and son. *The dramatic difference lies not in the perception of past and present, but in the anticipation of a specific hope for the future. There is a remarkable verse in the last of the prophets (Malachi 3: 24)* [this is my emphasis, and here is one of the archives which attest to that "anticipation of a specific hope for the future"—an archive, according to the archivist, which would be "unique"—the word is very serious] which expresses a *unique vision* [my emphasis] that is not to be found—*at least not explicitly* [I also emphasize this concession which opens onto the abyss which it denies]—in the messianic prophecies of any of his predecessors. All the others, we might say, posit an ultimate resolution of the Oedipal conflict between Israel and God; Malachi does so also on the level of the purely human: *"Ve-heshiv lev avot 'al banim ve-lev banim 'al avotam"* (He shall reconcile the heart of fathers with sons and the heart of sons with their fathers). [95]

More confident than I would be about the meaning here in all rigor of "unique," "explicitly," and "purely human," Yerushalmi continues—and this is the point of rupture:

> *Le-didakh.* Let it be according to you that religion, the great illusion, has no future. But what is the future of Laius and Oedipus? We read to the end of your *Moses,* and you do not say [thus, once again, Yerushalmi records a silence of Freud, who he will nonetheless make speak, virtually, not explicitly, in the conditional, in the very next sentence]. *But should you tell me that, indeed, they have no hope, I shall simply reply—you may very well*

be right. But it is on this question of hope or hopelessness, even more than on God or godlessness, that your teaching may be at its most un-Jewish. [95, my emphasis]

What would be the least Jewish, the most "un-Jewish," the most heterogeneous to Jewishness, would not be a lack of *Judaism, a distancing,* as the French translation says, *with respect to Judaism* (religion, belief in God, Israel's election), but the nonbelief in the future—that is to say, in what constitutes Jewishness *beyond all Judaism.*

Beyond the precautions and the conditions, we have here an affirmation which is excluded from all discussion to come, an unconditional affirmation: the link between Jewishness, if not Judaism, and hope in the future. This affirmation is unconditional, first of all, in its form: it is intractable and excludes itself, for what ties it to Jewishness, from all discussion. But it is again unconditional in its content, as should be every affirmation of this type. It is in effect nothing other than the affirmation of affirmation, the "yes" to the originary "yes," the inaugural engagement of a promise or of an anticipation which wagers, *a priori,* the very future. The necessity of affirming affirmation, the affirmation of affirmation, must be at once tautological and heterological. Yerushalmi is ready to make concessions on everything, including on the existence of God and on the future of religion, on everything except on the trait that links Jewishness and the opening toward the future. And, still more radically, on *the absolute uniqueness of this trait.* The uniqueness of the trait is first of all the *ineffaceable* hyphen, *trait d'union,* between Jewishness and future [*à-venir*]. The being-Jewish and the being-open-toward-the-future would be the same thing, the same unique thing, the same thing as uniqueness—and they would not be dissociable the one from the other. To be open toward the future would be to be Jewish. And vice versa. And in *exemplary* fashion. It would be not only to have a future, to be capable of anticipation, etc., a shared aptitude whose universality could appear to be indisputable, but to be in relation to the future *as such,* and to hold one's identity, reflect it, declare it, announce it to oneself, only out of what comes from the future to come. Thus would be the trait, the *exemplary* uniqueness of the *trait d'union.*

Without risking myself in the logical abyss of this affirmation and in the aporias of exemplarity, which I have tried to describe elsewhere, and indeed on the subject of Jewish exemplarity, I must once again content myself with pointing to the archive. Precisely where we see one door open or close upon another. Because in the last analysis, this unconditional affirmation, which presents itself, I said, as *ineffaceable,* bases its authority, in the first place, on the precedence of an archive—for example, as we just saw, a verse of the last of the prophets, as it is interpreted by the archivist. But the authority of the same unconditional affirmation is above all based on what could resemble another unique trait of Jewishness according to Yerushalmi, and which undoubtedly repeats the first as if it came down to the same thing. This time it has to do not only with opening toward the future, but with *historicity* and with the obligation of *memory,* or better, with the *obligation of the archive.* I am referring now to another of Yerushalmi's books, as fine and as rightly celebrated, *Zakhor: Jewish History and Jewish Memory.* If, in the passage of *Freud's Moses* we were just reading, Yerushalmi named the *drama* of a "dramatic difference" on the subject of the *future* as something Jewish, here he speaks again of *drama,* of "dramatic evidence" (dramatic proof, mark, clue, dramatic testimony, in the broad sense of the word "testimony," one could even say archive) on the subject of the *past* as something Jewish and *uniquely, exclusively, only Jewish:*

> No more dramatic evidence is needed for the dominant place of history in ancient Israel than the overriding fact that even God is known only insofar as he reveals himself "historically." [9]

And after several citations meant to support this affirmation in quotes, we find ourselves before this extraordinary attribution: the injunction of memory falls to Israel, and to Israel alone. Now a minute ago, already, we had the same attribution, the same assignation without any sharing. It was a question then of "the anticipation of a specific hope for the future." Two exclusivities, indeed two exclusions. Two solitudes and two responsibilities, two assignations in the absolute privilege of election. As if Yerushalmi were ready to renounce everything in Judaism (terminable) that was not

Jewishness (interminable), everything, the belief in the existence of God, the religion, the culture, etc., except that archived trait of Jewishness which is something that at least *resembles* election even if it is not to be confused with it: the absolute privilege, the absolute uniqueness in the experience of the promise (the future) and the injunction of memory (the past). But the two are not added or juxtaposed: the one is founded on the other. It is because there has been an archived event, because the injunction or the law has already presented and *inscribed* itself into historical memory as an injunction of memory, with or without substrate, that the two absolute privileges are bound the one to the other. As if God had inscribed only one thing into the memory of one *single people* and of an *entire people:* in the future, remember to remember the future. And as if the word "people," in this sentence, could only be conceived of out of the unprecedented uniqueness of this archive injunction. Here is what I call the extraordinary attribution, on the subject of which I will keep a large number of grave questions in reserve. Some of them would have an ethical or political dimension, but they are not the only ones, in spite of their obvious urgency. I would have liked to spend hours, in truth an eternity, meditating while trembling before this sentence:

> Only in Israel and nowhere else is the injunction to remember felt as a religious imperative to an entire people. [9]

How can one not tremble before this sentence?

I wonder if it is just. Who could ever be assured, by what archive, that it is just, this sentence? Just with the justice that Yerushalmi suggests so profoundly elsewhere could indeed be the opposite of forgetting? I feel myself to be very close to what he says then in this direction, and incidentally, in the form of a question.[14] At the end of the postscript of *Zakhor,* the same question in effect reso-

14. I have, for my part, notably in *Force de loi* and *Specters of Marx,* tried to situate justice, the justice which exceeds but also requires the law, in the direction of the act of memory, of resistance to forgetting, whether this be of the injunction in general or of its place of assignation: other people, living or dead.

nates. "Is it possible that the antonym of 'forgetting' is not 'remembering', but *justice?*" [117].

Thinking about this justice, I wonder, trembling, if they are just, the sentences which reserve for Israel *both* the future *and* the past *as such, both* hope ("the anticipation of a specific hope for the future") *and* the duty of memory ("the injuction to remember"), assignation which would be felt by Israel *alone,* Israel as a *people* and Israel in its *totality* ("only in Israel and nowhere else" "as a religious imperative to an entire people").

Unless, in the logic of this election, one were to call by the *unique* name of Israel all the places and all the peoples who would be ready to recognize themselves in this anticipation and in this injunction—and then this would no longer only be a vertiginous problem of semantics or of rhetoric. Like the question of the proper name, the question of exemplarity, which I put aside earlier, here situates the place of all violences. Because if it is just to remember the future and the injunction to remember, namely the archontic injunction to guard and to gather the archive, it is no less just to remember the others, the other others and the others in oneself, and that the other peoples could say the same thing—in another way. And that *tout autre est tout autre,* as we can say in French: every other is every other other, is altogether other.

Formalizing too quickly so as to gain time, let us go straight to the reason for which one can be dumbfounded with dread before the virtual injustice one risks committing in the name of justice itself. Let us formulate the argument drily in a mode which in a certain sense crosses psychoanalysis with deconstruction, a certain "psychoanalysis" and a certain "deconstruction." When I say that *I* tremble, I mean that *one* trembles, the "one" or the "*on*" trembles, whoever it is trembles: because the injustice of this justice can concentrate its violence in the very constitution of the *One* and of the *Unique.* Right where it can affect everyone, everyone and anyone, whoever. In the sentences I just cited, the words that make (me) tremble are only those that say the One, the difference of the One in the form of uniqueness ("dramatic difference," "unique vision," "specific hope," "Only in Israel and nowhere else") and the One in the figure of totalizing assemblage ("to an entire people"). The gathering into itself of the One is never without violence, nor is the self-affirmation of the Unique, the law of the archontic, the law of *consignation* which orders the archive. Consignation is never without that excessive pressure (impression, repression, suppression) of which repression (*Verdrängung* or *Urverdrängung*) and suppression (*Unterdrückung*) are at least figures.

For it may not be necessary to give psychoanalytic names to this violence. Neither necessary nor assured. Nor primordial. Is it not sufficient to recognize this violence at work in the archontic constitution of the One and of the Unique for Freud to find an automatic or structural justification for his "historical novel"? Does the necessity of this archontic violence not give meaning to his *Moses,* and even an undeniable truth, a "historical truth" if not a "material truth"? To *his* "Moses," to Jakob his father, in short to Freud, whose Moses was also the Moses of Yerushalmi? To the son as grandfather (to whomever, to any "one," to some*one* who says "I," to myself, for example, Jakob or Elie, I who have not only a father named Hayim, but also, as if by chance, a grandfather named Moses. And another, Abraham)?

As soon as there is the One, there is murder, wounding, traumatism. *L 'Un se garde de l' autre.* The One guards against/keeps some of the other. It protects *itself* from the other, but, in the movement of this jealous violence, it comprises in itself, thus guarding it, the self-otherness or self-difference (the difference from within oneself) which makes it One. The "One differing, deferring from itself." The One as the Other. At once, at the same time, but in a same time that is out of joint, the One forgets to remember itself to itself, it keeps and erases the archive of this injustice that it is. Of this violence that it does. *L'Un se fait violence.* The One makes itself violence. It violates and does violence to itself but it also institutes itself as violence. It becomes what it is, the very violence—that it does to itself. Self-determination as violence. *L'Un se garde de l' autre pour se faire violence* (*because* it makes itself violence and *so as* to make itself violence). Only in French can this be said and thus archived in such an *economical* fashion.[15]

---

15. At the end of this lecture, not without irony, I imagine, with as much depth as astonishment but, as always, with an intractable lucidity, Geoffrey

Now it is necessary that this repeat itself. It is Necessity itself, *Anankē*. The One, as self-repetition, can only repeat and recall this instituting violence. It can only affirm itself and engage itself in this repetition. This is even what ties in depth the injunction of memory with the anticipation of the future to come. The injunction, even when it summons memory or the safeguard of the archive, turns incontestably toward the future to come. It orders to promise, but it orders repetition, and first of all self-repetition, self-confirmation in a *yes, yes*. If repetition is thus inscribed at the heart of the future to come, one must also import there, *in the same stroke,* the death drive, the violence of forgetting, *superrepression* (suppression and repression), the anarchive, in short, the possibility of putting to death the very thing, whatever its name, which *carries the law in its tradition:* the archon of the archive, the table, *what* carries the table and *who* carries the table, the subjectile, the substrate, and the subject of the law.

This is why Freud might not have accepted in this form the alternative between the future and the past of Oedipus, or between "hope" and "hopelessness," the Jew and the non-Jew, the future and repetition. The one, alas, or happily, is the condition of the other. And the Other is the condition for the One. To be able to say that the decisive and for the moment undecidable question is

---

Bennington remarked to me that by underlining, and first by bringing into play, such an untranslatability, I risked repeating the gesture I seemed to put into question in the hands of the other, namely, the affirmation of the unique or of the idiom.

To clarify here the response I gave him then, I will briefly say three things:

1. I did not talk of *absolute* untranslatability or idiomaticity, but of a greater *economy* (it was a question of my saying in very few French words, *in this case, in this occurrence,* what can by all means be translated in any language, if only one uses more); which suffices to change the *political* sense of this gesture.

2. I believe that the affirmation of a certain idiomaticity, of a certain uniqueness, as of a certain *differing, deferring, that is to say, impure, unity* is irreducible and necessary—and I wanted thus to demonstrate it practically. What one does next, both with this affirmation, and with this impurity, is precisely where all of politics comes in.

3. Let us say at last that I wanted to exercise, in another political gesture, my own right to irony and, exposing myself to it thus in my language, to give an example of this fatal necessity and of its risks.

knowing, if at least it is a matter of knowledge ("if it is at all knowable"), what the words "Jewish" and "science" mean, and that this remains open toward the future, one must give oneself at least a preunderstanding of what "to come" means. Now it is in the structure of the future to come that it can only posit itself while welcoming repetition, as much in the respect for faithfulness—to others and to oneself—as in the violent re-positioning of the One. The answer to the question ("what is the future?") seems thus to be presupposed by Yerushalmi. It is prior to the affirmation according to which the future will say how to define "science" and "Jewish" and "Jewish science."

With respect to this presupposition or this preunderstanding, we find ourselves here before an aporia. I have attempted to struggle with this elsewhere, and I shall say only a word about it, from the point of view of the archive: does one base one's thinking of the future on an archived event—with or without substrate, with or without actuality—for example on a divine injunction or on a messianic covenant? Or else, on the contrary, can an *experience,* an *existence,* in general, only receive and record, only archive such an event to the extent that the structure of this existence and of its temporalization makes this archivization possible? In other words, does one need a first archive in order to conceive of originary archivability? Or vice versa? This is the whole question of the relation between the event of the religious revelation (*Offenbarung*) and a revealability (*Offenbarkeit*), a possibility of manifestation, the prior thought of what opens toward the arrival or toward the coming of such an event. Is it not true that the logic of the after-the-fact (*Nachträglichkeit*), which is not only at the heart of psychoanalysis, but even, literally, the sinews of all "deferred" (*nachträglich*) obedience, turns out to disrupt, disturb, entangle forever the reassuring distinction between the two terms of this alternative, as between the past and the future, that is to say, between the three actual presents, which would be the past present, the present present, and the future present?

In any case, there would be no future without repetition. And thus, as Freud might say (this would be his thesis), there is no future without the specter of the oedipal violence that inscribes the superrepression into the archontic institution of the archive, in the position, the auto-position or the hetero-position of the One and of the Unique, in the nomological *arkhē*. And the death drive. Without this evil, which is also *archive fever,* the desire and the disorder of the archive, there would be neither assignation nor consignation. For assignation is a consignation. And when one says nomological *arkhē,* one says *nomos,* one says the law, but also *thesis* or *themis.* The law of institution (*nomos, thesis,* or *themis*) is the *thesis. Thesis* and *themis* are sometimes, not always, in tension with the originary *physis,* with what one translates commonly as "nature."

It is thus that, with the thesis, the supplement of theses that were to follow the *Exergue, Preamble,* and *Foreword* has insinuated itself *already and in advance.* That is, not to resist the desire of a postscript, a prosthesis on Freud's theses.[16] Which is advanced at the pace of other ghosts.

16. Freud does not hesitate to speak of a *prosthesis* of repression. Certain "adjuvant and substitutive technologies" prove that "the fulfillment of repression in its regular form comes up against difficulties." But this sign of failure also permits to better "illuminate," *right on* the prosthesis, the "end" and the "technique" of repression. All of this concerns the event itself, the coming of what arrives—or not. There is nothing fortuitous in that one of these prostheses serves the *ungeschehenmachen,* the "making it not have happened," even though it has happened. It is thus to "treat an event as 'not happened'" (in French in the text: "non arrivé") [see "Inhibitions, Symptoms and Anxiety," 20:77].

Theses

Vienna, 6 December 1896
. . . I have now adorned my room with plaster casts of Florentine statues. It was a source of extraordinary invigoration for me. I am thinking of getting rich, in order to be able to repeat these trips. A congress on Italian soil!
(Naples, Pompeii).

> Most cordial greetings
> to you all,
> Your
> Sigm.[17]

A young archaeologist, Norbert Hanold, had discovered in a museum of antiquities in Rome a relief which had so immensely attracted him that he was greatly pleased at obtaining an excellent plaster cast of it which he could hang in his study. . . .[18]

I have long grown used to being dead.[19]

17. Letter to Wilhelm Fliess (6 December 1896) [*Complete Letters* 214]. These words conclude a long letter in which Freud defines the relations of topographic, archaeological, or archival "stratification" among several types of "recording" ("three and probably more," he thinks then). This letter prefigures the "Note on the 'Mystic Writing-Pad,'" at times in the details [*SE* 19: 227–32].

18. Freud, *Delusions and Dreams in Jensen's "Gradiva"* (1906–07) [*SE* 9: 10]. We will quote this translation henceforth, occasionally modifying it.

19. "Ich habe mich schon lange daran gewöhnt, tot zu sein." Jensen, *Gradiva,* cited by Freud.

Let us pretend to recapitulate—where a *recapitulation* seems impossible, when nothing any longer can reunite itself right in close to the head, to the principle, to the arkhē, or to the archive. Let us thus recall the idiomatic formulas which we claimed could only print themselves so economically in the French language. They express archive fever. *L'Un se garde de l'autre,* we said. And *l'Un se fait violence. L'Un se garde de l'autre pour se faire violence* (the One keeps (from) the other *for* making itself violence): *because* it makes itself violence and *so as to* make itself violence.

In another language altogether, is this not what Freud would perhaps have replied? Is this not, in substance, what Freud's specter for which no one here wants to be substituted would perhaps have declared to Yerushalmi? So the father of psychoanalysis—and of Anna—did not take into consideration the question concerning what his daughter in effect wrote, in his name or in her name (the content of the response to such a question was already archived, at least in the letter to Enrico Morselli, as early as 1926). But he did perhaps respond in that way, in the form of an ellipsis, to the question of the *future* of an illusion, in sum. The question of the future of the specter or the specter of the future, of the future *as specter.*

Who wants to substitute him- or herself for Freud's phantom? How can one not want to, as well? The moment has perhaps come to risk, in a few telegrams, a thesis on the subject of Freud's theses. The thesis would first say this: all the Freudian theses are cleft, divided, contradictory, as are the concepts, beginning with that of the archive. Thus it is for every concept: always dislocating itself because it is never one with itself. It is the same with the thesis which posits and arranges the concepts, the history of concepts, their formation as much as their archivization.

Why stress spectrality here? Because Yerushalmi dared to address Freud's phantom? Because he had the audacity to ask him for a confidential response whose archive he would never unveil? Undoubtedly, but in the first place because the structure of the archive is *spectral.* It is spectral *a priori:* neither present nor absent "in the flesh," neither visible nor invisible, a trace always referring to another whose eyes can never be met, no more than those of Hamlet's father, thanks to the possibility of a visor. Also, the spectral motif stages this disseminating fission from which the archontic principle, and the concept of the archive, and the concept in general suffer, from the principle on.

It is known that Freud did everything possible to not neglect the experience of haunting, spectrality, phantoms, ghosts. He tried to account for them. Courageously, in as scientific, critical, and positive a fashion as possible. But by doing that, he also tried to conjure them. Like Marx. His scientific positivism was put to the service of his declared hauntedness and of his unavowed fear. Let us take only one example. I shall choose it from up close to archive desire, from up close to an impossible archaeology of this nostalgia, of this painful desire for a return to the authentic and singular origin, and for a return concerned to account for the desire to return: for itself. This example calls me back close to Naples and to Pompeii, in the landscape of Gradiva, where I wrote these pages some ten days ago.

In his reading of Jensen's *Gradiva,* Freud avows being himself haunted. He denies it without denying it, he defends himself without defending himself. He fends himself, if you will, at the moment he wants to account for the last evolution of Hanold's insanity (*Wahn*), the haunted insanity of someone else—and of someone else as a character in fiction. The latter thinks that he speaks for a whole hour with Gradiva, with his "mid-day ghost" (*Mittags-gespenst*), though she has been buried since the catastrophe of 79. He *monologues with* Gradiva's ghost for an hour, then the latter regains her tomb, and Hanold, the archaeologist, remains alone. But he also remains duped by the hallucination.

What will Freud do? He had first clearly posed the classical problem of the phantom. And of the phantom in literature. The "character" is not the only one to be ill at ease or to suffer from a "tension" (*Spannung*). Faced with the "apparition of Gradiva," we ask ourselves in the first place, we the readers, *who it is,* for we have first seen her in the form of a stone statue, and then of a fantastical image (*Phantasiebild*). The hesitation does not oscillate simply between the phantom and reality, effective reality (*wirkliche*). Putting it in quotation marks, Freud speaks of a "'real' ghost" (*ein "wirk-liches" Gespenst*): "Is she a hallucination of our hero, led astray by his delusions? Is she a 'real' ghost? or a living person [*leibhaftige Person*]?" [17]. To ask oneself these questions, Freud notes, one does not need to "believe in ghosts." The question and the "tension" it engenders are only more inevitable in that Jensen, the author of what he himself calls a "fantastic fiction" (*Phantasiestück*), has not yet explained to us whether he wanted to leave us in our prosaic mode or if he wanted to "transport us into another and imaginary world, in which spirits and ghosts [*Geister und Gespenster*] are given reality [*Wirklichkeit*]" [17, my emphasis]. We are prepared to "follow" the author of fiction as in "the examples of *Hamlet* and *Macbeth*."

Let us never forget it: at midday, at the "hour of ghosts" (*Geisterstunde*), Gradiva, the "mid-day ghost," appears for us in an experience of *reading,* but also, for the hero of the novel, in an experience the *language* of which, indeed the multiplicity of languages, cannot be abstracted away to leave naked pure perception or even a purely perceptive hallucination. Hanold also addresses himself to Gradiva in Greek to see if the spectral existence (*Scheindasein*) has retained the power to speak (*Sprachvermögen*). Without response, he then addresses her in Latin. She smiles and asks him to speak in his own proper idiom, German: "If you want to speak to me, you must do it in German." A phantom can thus be sensitive to idiom. Welcoming to this one, allergic to that one. One does not address it in just any language. It is a law of economy, once again, a law of the *oikos,* of the transaction of signs and values, but also of some familial domesticity: haunting implies places, a habitation, and always a haunted house.

This economy is no longer separated from questions of "effectivity," thus in quotations: is a phantom "real" (*wirklich*) or not? But also of "truth." What about the truth for Freud, faced with these specters? What, in his eyes, is the share, the allowance, the part of truth? Because he believes in something like a *part* of the truth. He tells us that under analysis, under psychoanalytic examination, this delusion's lack of verisimilitude (*die Unwahrscheinlichkeit dieses Wahnes*) seems to dissipate (*scheint . . . zu zergehen*), at least to a large extent: "the greater part [*zum grösseren Teile*]" [70].

So here is a lack of verisimilitude which seems to dissipate with explication, *at least in large part!* What is this part? What is it due to, this piece which resists explanation? Why this insistence on the part, the parting, the partition, the piece? And what does this partition have to do with the truth?

We know the Freudian explanation. Announced by this strange protocol, it mobilizes the whole etiological machinery of psychoanalysis, beginning, obviously, with the mechanisms of repression. But we should not forget that if the psychoanalytic explanation of delusion, of hauntedness, of hallucination, if the psychoanalytic theory of specters, in sum, leaves a part, a share of nonverisimilitude unexplained or rather *verisimilar,* carrying truth, this is because, and Freud recognizes it himself a bit further on, there is a *truth of delusion,* a truth of insanity or of hauntedness. Analogous to that "historical truth" which Freud distinguishes, notably in *Moses,* from the "material truth," this truth is repressed or suppressed. But it resists and *returns,* as such, as the spectral truth of delusion or of hauntedness. It *returns,* it belongs, it comes down to spectral truth. Delusion or insanity, hauntedness is not only haunted by this or that ghost, Gravida for example, but by the specter of the truth which has been thus repressed. The truth is spectral, and this is its part of truth which is irreducible by explanation.

A bit further on, Freud attempts again to allow for, to account for this part in the hallucinatory haunting of the archaeologist:

> If a patient believes in his delusion so firmly, this is not because [*so geschieht das nicht*] his faculty of judgement has been overturned and does not arise from what is false [*irrig ist*] in the delusion. On the contrary, there is a grain of truth concealed in every delusion [*Sondern in jedem Wahn steckt auch ein Körnchen Wahrheit*], there is something in it that really deserves belief [*es ist etwas an ihm, was wirklich den Glauben verdient*], and this is the source [*die Quelle*] of the patient's conviction, which is therefore to that extent justified [*der also so weit berechtigten Überzeugung des Kranken*]. This true element [*dieses Wahre,* this truth, the truth's seed of truth], however, has long been repressed [*war lange Zeit verdrängt*]. If eventually it is able to penetrate into consciousness, this time in a distorted form [*in entstelleter Form*], the sense of conviction attaching to it is over-intensified as though by way of compensation and is now attached to the distorted

substitute of the repressed truth [*am Entstellungsersatz des ver-drängten Wahren*]. [80]

To decipher the archive of this score, to read its truth right on the monument of this portion, one must take into account a *prosthesis,* this "distorted substitute." But a part of truth remains, a piece or a grain of truth breathes at the heart of the delusion, of the illusion, of the hallucination, of the hauntedness. This is a figure we find again literally in *Moses,* precisely when Freud distinguishes "historical" truth from "material" truth. For example: if Moses was the first Messiah, and Christ was his *prosthetic substitute* (Ersatzmann), his representative and his successor, in this case, Saint Paul was in a certain sense justified to address the nations as he did (*konnte auch Paulus mit einer gewissen historischen Berechtigung den Völkern zurufen*) to tell them that the Messiah had in effect come (*wirklich gekommen*) and that he was put to death "before your eyes" (*vor Euren Augen*). "Then, too," Freud says, "there is an element of historical truth in Christ's resurrection [literally, a piece of historical truth: *ein Stück historischer Wahrheit*], for he was the resurrected Moses and behind him the returned primal father [*Urvater*] of the primitive horde, transfigured and, as the son, put in the place of the father" [90].

Having thus accounted for the part of truth, taken care to isolate the seed of truth in the hallucination of the archaeologist who is prey to the "mid-day ghost," Freud means to confirm this truth of revisitation. He wants to demonstrate while illustrating. With the art of manipulating its suspense, like a narrator or like the author of a fiction, he tells us, in turn, a story. But as if it were the history of someone else, a case. Not the case of a patient, but the case of a doctor. "I know of a doctor," he says [*SE* 9:71]. The doctor had seen a ghost. He had witnessed the spectral return of a dead person and he could, in sum, bear witness to it. Freud had just noted that the belief in spirits, in specters, and in returning souls (*der Glaube an Geister und Gespenster und wiederkehrende Seelen*) should not be taken as a survival, a simple residue of religion and of childhood. The experience in which we meet specters or let them come visit us remains indestructible and undeniable. The most cultivated, the most reasonable, the most nonbelieving people easily reconcile a

certain spiritualism with reason. We know about the Freudian in-
trigue on the subject of telepathy. I tried to discuss this elsewhere,
in a more or less fictional fashion, and I will not go back into it.
What is at issue here is an analogous problematic. Freud wants to
teach with the aid of an example: "*Ich weiss von einem Arzt,*" "I
know a doctor . . ." And he tells us, as if it had to do with someone
else, the misadventure of a colleague. The latter reproached himself for a professional imprudence: it may have led to the death of
one of his patients. Many years later, he sees a young girl enter his
office. He recognizes the dead person. He tells himself then that it
is "true [*wahr*] that the dead can come back [*dass tie Toten wieder-
kommen können*]" [71]. His hallucination had been favored, it was
lucky, if you will: the specter presented itself as the sister of the
deceased women and also suffered from Graves' disease.

Here is the *coup de théâtre,* the dramatic twist. Freud pretended
to speak of someone else, of a colleague. (If I were to be immodest
to such a point, doubly immodest, I would say that he did what I
am doing in speaking of a colleague, Yerushalmi, while I am speaking of myself.) Freud presents himself, he says, in sum "here I am":
"*Der Arzt aber, dem sich dies ereignet, war ich selbt* . . . ," "The doctor
to whom this occurred was, however, none other than myself . . ."
[72]. And he does not fail to draw a conclusion: he is in a good
position not to refuse Hanold the archaeologist the *clinical possibility* of a brief delusion, but also the *right* to a furtive hallucination.
As soon as a semi-specter appears, it is also the right of manifestation of a certain truth (which is a bit spectral, *in part* spectral) in
the person of a sort of *species* of "real phantom." The *species,* the
aspect, the *specter,* this is what remains to be seen with the truth,
what is needed to speculate with the true of that truth.

In the end, Yerushalmi is right. He has managed to allow for
truth's part. Freud had his ghosts, he confesses it on occasion. He
lets us partake in his truth. He had his, and he obeyed them (Jakob
Shelomoh, Moses, and a few others), as does Yerushalmi (Jakob
Shelomoh, Sigmund Shelomoh, his Moses, and a few others), and
I myself (Jakob, Hayim, my grandfathers Moses and Abraham,
and a few others).

Freud's discourse on the archive, and here is the thesis of the
theses, seems thus to be divided. As does his concept of the archive.

It takes two contradictory forms. That is why we say, and this declaration can always translate an avowal, *archive fever.* One should be able to find traces of this contradiction in all Freud's works. This contradiction is not negative, it modulates and conditions the very formation of the concept of the archive and of the concept in general—right where they bear the contradiction.

If Freud suffered from *mal d'archive,* if his case stems from a *trouble de l'archive,* he is not without his place, simultaneously, in the archive fever or disorder we are experiencing today, concerning its lightest symptoms or the great holocaustic tragedies of our modern history and historiography: concerning all the detestable revisionisms, as well as the most legitimate, necessary, and courageous rewritings of history. Before gathering and formalizing the double Freudian postulation about the archive, I would like to justify the French expressions I just used: the *trouble de l'archive* and the *mal d'archive.*

Nothing is less reliable, nothing is less clear today than the word "archive." And not only because of the two orders of the *arkhē* we distinguished at the beginning. Nothing is more troubled and more troubling. The trouble with what is troubling here is undoubtedly what troubles and muddles our vision (as they say in French), what inhibits sight and knowledge, but also the trouble of troubled and troubling affairs (as they also say in French), the trouble of secrets, of plots, of clandestineness, of half-private, half-publlic conjurations, always at the unstable limit between public and private, between the family, the society, and the State, between the family and an intimacy even more private than the family, between oneself and oneself. I thus name the *trouble,* or what is called in English the "trouble," of these visions and of these affairs in a French idiom that is again untranslatable, to recall at least that the archive always holds a problem for translation. With the irreplaceable singularity of a document to interpret, to repeat, to reproduce, but each time in its original uniqueness, an archive ought to be idiomatic, and thus at once offered and unavailable for translation, open to and shielded from technical iteration and reproduction.

Nothing is thus more troubled and more troubling today than the concept archived in this word "archive." What is more probable, on the other hand, and more clear, is that psychoanalysis is not without responsibility in this trouble. It wants to analyze it, but it also heightens it. In naming psychoanalysis here, one refers already, in any case, to the archive which is classified, at least provisionally, under the name of "psychoanalysis," of "Freud," and of a few others. In other words, if we no longer know very well what we are saying when we say "archive," "Freud" is undoubtedly not without responsibility. But the name of Freud, the name of the Freuds, as we have seen, itself becomes plural, thus problematic.

The *trouble de l'archive* stems from a *mal d'archive.* We are *en mal d'archive:* in need of archives. Listening to the French idiom, and in it the attribute *en mal de,* to be *en mal d'archive* can mean something else than to suffer from a sickness, from a trouble or from what the noun *mal* might name. It is to burn with a passion. It is never to rest, interminably, from searching for the archive right where it slips away. It is to run after the archive, even if there's too much of it, right where something in it anarchives itself. It is to have a compulsive, repetitive, and nostalgic desire for the archive, an irrepressible desire to return to the origin, a homesickness, a nostalgia for the return to the most archaic place of absolute commencement. No desire, no passion, no drive, no compulsion, indeed no repetition compulsion, no *"mal-de"* can arise for a person who is not already, in one way or another, *en mal d'archive.* Now the principle of the internal division of the Freudian gesture, and thus of the Freudian concept of the archive, is that at the moment when psychoanalysis formalizes the conditions of archive fever and of the archive itself, it repeats the very thing it resists or which it makes its object. It raises the stakes. Such is the case with the *three plus one* theses (or prostheses). Three of them have to do with the concept of the archive, one other with the concept of concept.

1. First thesis and first surenchère *(higher bid)*

On the one hand, in effect, with the single but decisive conception of a topic of the psychic apparatus (and thus of repression or of suppression, according to the places of inscription, both inside and outside), Freud made possible the idea of an archive properly speaking, of a hypomnesic or technical archive, of the substrate or the subjectile (material or virtual) which, in what is already a psychic *spacing,* cannot be reduced to memory: neither to memory as conscious reserve, nor to memory as rememoration, as act of recalling. The psychic archive comes neither under *mnēmē* nor under *anamnēsis.*

But *on the other hand,* as I tried to show in "Freud and the Scene of Writing," this does not stop Freud, as classical metaphysician, from holding the technical prosthesis to be a secondary and accessory exteriority. In spite of resorting to what he holds to be a model of auxiliary representation, he invariably maintains a primacy of live memory and of anamnesis in their originary temporalization. From which we have the archaeological outbidding by which psychoanalysis, in its archive fever, always attempts to return to the live origin of that which the archive loses while keeping it in a multiplicity of places. As we have noted all along, there is an incessant tension here between the archive and archaeology. They will always be close the one to the other, resembling each other, hardly discernible in their co-implication, and yet radically incompatible, *heterogeneous,* that is to say, *different with regard to the origin,* in *divorce with regard to the arkhē.* Now Freud was incessantly tempted to redirect the original interest he had for the psychic archive toward archaeology (the word *"archiv,"* by the way, appears already in the *Studies on Hysteria* (1895) [*SE* 2]).[20] The scene of excavation, the theater of archaeological digs are the preferred places of this brother to Hanold. Each time he wants to teach the topology of archives, that is to say, of what ought to exclude or forbid the return to the origin, this lover of stone figurines proposes archaeological parables. The most remarkable and the most precocious of them is well known, in the study of hysteria of 1896. We must once again underline a few words in this work to mark what is to my eyes the most acute moment. A moment and not a process, this instant does not belong to the laborious deciphering of the archive. It is the nearly ecstatic instant Freud dreams of, when the very success of the dig must sign the effacement of the archivist: *the origin then speaks by itself.* The *arkhē* appears in the nude, without archive. It

20. As I was reminded after the lecture by Dany Nobus, whom I thank, the same word also appears in *Zum psychischen Mechanismus des Vergesslichkeit* (1898).

presents itself and comments on itself by itself. "Stones talk!" In the present. *Anamnēsis* without *hypomnēsis!* The archaeologist has succeeded in making the archive no longer serve any function. It *comes to efface itself,* it becomes transparent or unessential so as to let the *origin* present itself in person. Live, without mediation and without delay. Without even the memory of a translation, once the intense work of translation has succeeded. And this would be the "advance" of an "anamnesis." The time Freud consecrates to this long voyage in a field of excavations also says something of a *jouissance.* He would like it to be interminable, he prolongs it under the pretext of pedagogy or rhetoric:

> But in order to explain the relationship between the method which we have to employ for this purpose and the older method of *anamnestic* enquiry, I should like to bring before you an analogy taken from an advance that has in fact been made in another field of work.
>
> Imagine that an employer arrives in a little-known region where his interest is aroused by an expanse of ruins, with remains of walls, fragments of columns, and tablets with half-effaced and unreadable inscriptions. He may content himself with inspecting what lies exposed to view, with questioning the inhabitants—perhaps semi-barbaric people—who live in the vicinity, about what tradition tells them of the history and meaning of these archaeological remains, and with noting down what they tell him—and he may then proceed on his journey. But he may act differently. He may have brought picks, shovels and spades with him, and he may set the inhabitants to work with these implements. Together with them he may start upon the ruins, clear away the rubbish, and, beginning from the visible remains, uncover what is buried. *If his work is crowned with success, the discoveries are self-explanatory:* the ruined walls are part of the ramparts of a palace or a treasure-house; the fragments of columns can be filled out into a temple; the numerous inscriptions, which, by good luck, may be bilingual, reveal an alphabet and a language, and, when they have been deciphered and translated, yield undreamed-of information about the events of the remote past, to commemorate which the monuments were built.

Saxa loquuntur! ["The Aetiology of Hysteria" (1896), *SE* 3:192, my emphasis] [21]

2. Second thesis and second surenchère *(higher bid)*

On the one hand, the archive is made possible by the death, aggression, and destruction drive, that is to say also by originary finitude and expropriation. But beyond finitude as limit, there is, as we said above, this properly *in-finite* movement of radical destruction without which no archive desire or fever would happen. All the texts in the family and of the period of *Beyond the Pleasure Principle* explain in the end why there is archivization and why anarchiving destruction belongs to the process of archivization and produces the very thing it reduces, on occasion to ashes, and beyond.

But *on the other hand,* in the same moment, as classical metaphysician and as positivist *Aufklärer,* as critical scientist of a past epoch, as a "scholar" who does not want to speak with phantoms, Freud claims not to believe in death and above all in the virtual existence of the spectral space which he nonetheless takes into account. He takes it into account so as to account for it, and he intends to account for it or prove it right only while reducing it to something other than himself, that is to say, to something other than the other. He wants to explain and reduce the belief in the phantom. He wants to think through the grain of truth of this belief, but he believes that one cannot not believe in them and that one ought not to believe in them. Belief, the radical phenomenon of believing, the only relationship possible to the other as other, does not in the end have any possible place, any irreducible status in Freudian psychoanalysis. Which it nonetheless makes possible. From which we have the archaeological outbidding of a return to the reality, here to the originary effectivity of a base of immediate perception. A more profound and safer base than that of Hanold the archaeologist. Even more archaeological. The paradox takes on a striking, properly hallucinatory, form at the moment Freud sees himself obliged to let the phantoms speak for the duration of the archaeo-

94

21. Further on, the parable becomes a "comparison . . . with the excavation of a stratified ruined site" [3: 198].

logical digs but finishes by exorcising them in the moment he at last says, the work having been terminated (or supposed to have been), "Stones talk!" He believes he has exorcised them in the instant he lets them talk, provided that these specters talk, he believes, in the figurative. Like stones, nothing but that . . .

3. Third thesis and third surenchère (higher bid)

On the one hand, no one has illuminated better than Freud what we have called the archontic principle of the archive, which in itself presupposes not the originary *arkhē* but the nomological *arkhē* of the law, of institution, of domiciliation, of filiation. No one has analyzed, that is also to say, deconstructed, the authority of the archontic principle better than he. No one has shown how this archontic, that is, paternal and patriarchic, principle only posited itself to repeat itself and returned to re-posit itself only in parricide. It amounts to repressed or suppressed parricide, in the name of the father as dead father. The archontic is at best the takeover of the archive by the brothers. The equality and the liberty of brothers. A certain, still vivacious idea of democracy.

But *on the other hand,* in life as in his works, in his theoretical theses as in the compulsion of his institutionalizing strategy, Freud repeated the patriarchal logic. He declared, notably in *The Rat Man,* that the patriarchal right (*Vaterrecht*) marked the civilizing progress of reason. He even added to it in a patriarchic higher bid, even where all his inheritors, the psychoanalysts of all countries, have united themselves as a single man to follow him and to raise the stakes. To the point that certain people can wonder if, decades after his death, his sons, so many brothers, can yet speak in their own name. Or if his daughter ever came to life (*zōē*), was ever anything other than a phantasm or a specter, a Gradiva *rediviva,* a Gradiva-Zoe-Bertgang passing through at Berggasse 19.

Postscript

By chance, I wrote these last words on the rim of Vesuvius, right near Pompeii, less than eight days ago. For more than twenty years, each time I've returned to Naples, I've thought of her.

Who better than Gradiva, I said to myself this time, the *Gradiva* of Jensen and of Freud, could illustrate this outbidding in the *mal d'archive*? Illustrate it where it is no longer proper to Freud and to this concept of the archive, where it marks in its very structure (and this is a last *supplementary thesis*) the formation of every concept, the very history of conception?

When he wants to explain the haunting of the archaeologist with a logic of repression, at the very moment in which he specifies that he wants to recognize in it a germ or a parcel of truth, Freud claims again to bring to light a more originary origin than that of the specter. In the outbidding, he wants to be an archivist who is more of an archaeologist than the archaeologist. And, of course, closer to the ultimate cause, a better etiologist than his novelist. He wants to exhume a more archaic *impression,* he wants to exhibit a more archaic *imprint* than the one the other archaeologists of all kinds bustle around, those of literature and those of classical objective science, an imprint that is singular each time, an impression that is almost no longer an archive but almost confuses itself with the pressure of the footstep that leaves its still-living mark on a substrate, a surface, a place of origin. When the step is still one with the subjectile. In the instant when the printed archive is yet to be detached from the primary impression in its singular, irreproducible, and archaic origin. In the instant when the imprint is yet to be left, abandoned by the pressure of the impression. In the instant of the pure auto-affection, in the indistinction of the active and the passive, of a touching and the touched. An archive which would in sum confuse itself with the *arkhē,* with the origin of which it is only the *type,* the *typos,* the iterable letter or character. An archive without archive, where, suddenly indiscernible from the impression of its imprint, Gradiva's footstep speaks by itself! Now this is exactly what Hanold dreamed of in his disenchanted archaeologist's desire, in the moment when he awaited the coming of the "mid-day ghost."

Hanold suffers from archive fever. He has exhausted the science of archaeology. He had, the novel says, become a master in the art of deciphering the most indecipherable, the most enigmatic graffiti (*in der Entzifferung schwer enträtselbarer graffiti*). But he had had enough of his science and of his abilities. His impatient desire rebelled against their positivity as if before death. This science itself was of the past. What it taught, he said to himself, is a lifeless archaeological intuition (*eine leblose archäologische Anschauung*). And in the moment when Pompeii comes back to life, when the dead awake (*die Toten wachten auf, und Pompeji fing an, wieder zu leben*), Hanold understands everything. He understands why he had traveled through Rome and Naples. He begins to *know* (*wissen*) what he did not then know, namely his "intimate drive" or "impulse." And this knowledge, this comprehension, this deciphering of the interior desire to decipher which drove him on to Pompeii, all of this comes back to him in an act of memory (*Erinnerung*). He recalls that he came to see if he could find her traces, the traces of Gradiva's footsteps (*ob er hier Spuren von ihr auffinden könne*).

Now here is a point which is never taken into account, neither in Jensen's reading nor in Freud's, and this point confounds more than it distinguishes: Hanold has come to search for these traces in the literal sense (*im wörtlichen Sinne*). He dreams of bringing back to life. He dreams rather of reliving. But of reliving the other. Of reliving the singular pressure or impression which Gradiva's step [*pas*], the step itself, the step of Gradiva herself, that very day, at that time, on that date, in what was inimitable about it, must have left in the ashes. He dreams this irreplaceable place, the very ash, where the singular imprint, like a signature, barely distinguishes itself from the impression. And this is the condition of singularity, the idiom, the secret, testimony. It is the condition for the uniqueness of the printer-printed, of the impression and the imprint, of the pressure and its trace in the unique *instant* where they are not yet distinguished the one from the other, forming in an *instant* a single body of Gradiva's step, of her gait, of her pace (*Gangart*), and of the ground which carries them. The trace no longer distinguishes itself from its substrate. No longer distinguishing *between themselves,* this pressure and this imprint differ henceforth *from all other* impressions, from all other imprints, and from all other archives. At least that imprint (*Abdruck*), distinct from all the others, must be rediscovered—but this presupposes *both* memory *and* the archive, the one and the other as the same, *right on the same* subjectile in the field of excavations. It must be resuscitated right where, in an absolutely safe location, in an irreplaceable place, it still holds, right on the ash, not yet having detached itself, the pressure of Gradiva's so singular step.

This is what Hanold the archaeologist means in a literal sense by the *literal sense.* "In the literal sense" (*im wörtlichen Sinne*), the story says:

Something "came into his consciousness for the first time [*zum ersten mal*]: without being aware himself of the impulse within him, he had come to Italy and had traveled on to Pompeii, without stopping in Rome or Naples, in order to see whether he could find any traces of her. And 'traces' in the literal sense [*im wörtlichen Sinne*]; for with her peculiar gait she must have left behind an imprint [*Abdruck*] of her toes in the ashes distinct from all the rest." [*SE* 9:65, trans. modified] [22]

| 99

22. " . . . im wörtlichen Sinne, denn bei ihrer besonderen Gangart musste sie in der Ashe einen von allen übrigen sich unterscheidenden Abdruck der Zehen hinterlassen haben."

This uniqueness does not resist. Its price is infinite. But infinite in the immense, incommensurable extent to which it remains unfindable. The possibility of the archiving trace, this simple *possibility,* can only divide the uniqueness. Separating the impression from the imprint. Because this uniqueness is not even a past present. It would have been possible, one can dream of it after the fact, only insofar as its iterability, that is to say, its immanent divisibility, the possibility of its fission, haunted it from the origin. The faithful memory of such a singularity can only be given over to the specter.

Is fiction outdone here? Does it lack knowledge? Did Jensen know less about this than Freud? [23] And Hanold?

One can always dream or speculate around this secret account. Speculation begins there—and belief. But of the secret itself, there can be no archive, by definition. The secret is the very ash of the archive, the place where it no longer even makes sense to say "the very ash [*la cendre même*]" or "right on the ash [*à même la cendre*]." There is no sense in searching for the secret of what anyone may have known. *A fortiori* a character, Hanold the archaeologist.

That is what this literature attests. So here is a singular testimony, literature itself, an inheritor escaped—or emancipated—from the Scriptures. Here is what it gives us to think: the inviolable

---

23. It is known that Freud did not fail to take up this question. With a strategy at times disconcerting, he does justice to it in its general form on more than one occasion, but also with this example here in his text on Jensen's *Gradiva*. Because Jensen, as he notes, proposes an etiology and a genealogy of Hanold's "delusion." Do they hold up in the face of science? After having proposed, in a provocative and deliberately surprising fashion, to reverse the terms (it is science that does not hold up in the face of fiction), Freud complicates things. He proposes to ally himself, as the scholar of a new science, and much better armed, with the novelist. The latter will not be alone if "I may count my own works as part of science," Freud says, and if he can leave his provisional isolation. A note from 1912 remarks that this isolation is coming to an end: " . . . the 'psycho-analytic movement' started by me has become widely extended, and it is constantly growing" [*SE* 9:53]. The same question is set out from another point of view in chapter 4, which ends at the edge of an obvious fact forgotten along the way: "But we must stop here, or we may really forget that Hanold and Gradiva are only creatures of their author's mind" [*SE* 9:93]. Elsewhere, from another point of view, we will take up these texts and these questions of metainterpretative outbidding.

secret of *Gradiva*, of Hanold, of Jensen, and then of Freud—and of a few others. Beyond every possible and necessary inquiry, we will always wonder what Freud (for example), what every "careful concealer" may have wanted to keep secret. We will wonder what he may have kept of his unconditional right to secrecy, while at the same time burning with the desire to know, to make known, and to archive the very thing he concealed forever. What was concealed? What did he conceal even beyond the intention to conceal, to lie, or to perjure?

We will always wonder what, in this *mal d'archive,* he may have burned. We will always wonder, sharing with compassion in this archive fever, what may have burned of his secret passions, of his correspondence, or of his "life." Burned without him, without remains and without knowledge. With no possible response, be it spectral or not, short of or beyond a suppression, on the other edge of repression, originary or secondary, without a name, without the least symptom, and without even an ash.

Naples, 22–28 May 1994

TRANSLATOR'S NOTE
Eric Prenowitz

Right on
[à même]

Il faut traduire et il faut ne pas traduire.[1]

Customs officer, judge and executor, mountebank medium, impassive impostor, forger of authority, illiberal host and ungracious guest, the translator should never really be there.

Here's another way of saying the same thing: a translator's task is giving up. Rendering, and very often rending, each time wrenching. Caught in an intractable double bind, immemorial and infinitely iterated, one must decide or rule, *il faut trancher,* right where the idiomatic snarl won't be untied. It means giving up the dream of an effortless and silent living transfusion, immediate and unmitigated, unmediated. Giving up giving, in other words, because in the first place the thing does not belong to you and in the second it will not in any case have been handed over intact.

But giving, nonetheless. Getting and begetting. Forgiving, perhaps forgiven. Giving forgetting too.

And yet translation is so eminently plausible; what's more it happens all the time. A mechanical game of correspondences, in sum, an inexorable machine. Because nothing escapes, there's not a

1. *D'un ton apocalyptique adopté naguère en philosophie* (Paris: Galilée, 1983), p. 10.

single word that can't be taken, by ruse or by force. Which does not mean that all translations are equally faithful or captivating. There are inevitably trade-offs along the way and never an end in sight. Set in motion, the mutational process stops for no one. So while its transgressive lure may be formally irresistible, there is no definitive translation, by definition. At some point one simply has to give up. Period.

Things are hardly better for the reader, of course.

Willy-nilly, and *mutatis mutandis,* a translation's readers are inscribed into a position of "absolute dissymmetry and heteronomy" (p. 41) as Derrida says of a boy being circumcised, of Freud's phantom to whom Yerushalmi proclaims "I shall say 'we,'" and of anyone addressed by anyone else: you read something you cannot read, in any case something you will not have read once you're done reading. Like an infant who can neither comprehend nor respond. And while an author may be a reader's ghost, in translation the text itself is presented without being present: it is here and yet there. A translation is irresponsible, unreliable, deceptive. Yet imposing. Authoritarian if not authoritative. It inevitably inflicts an irresistible covenant. Whereas a foreign text in the *original* leaves the reader free, because the reader is not a reader, the text being foreign and thus legibly illegible for those who have not domesticated the other mother tongue. It does not suppose and impose a *we,* because to begin with it says "we" differently, that is, it literally does not say "we." Rather, and precisely because translation always remains possible, it inscribes the limits, the singularity or the extra-ordinary common to any *we.* And so a translation does violence at once to the text to which it offers an ambiguous hospitality, both becking and balking, and to the reader: it takes something foreign and makes something familiar, readable at least, and thereby imposes the indubitable community of a homolinguistic, a homonolinguistic *we.*

Here, these violences can perhaps be excused, for we must read Derrida, and well. However, they tend to conceal another one that is more pernicious while not wholly unpropitious: whatever it may change, a translation maintains above all *its own fiction,* it maintains the true fiction that translation is possible. It *is* this fiction, both hopeful and frightening, promising communication where none by definition should be possible, and simultaneously eliminating the possible communication of difference itself so to speak, regarding difference, or of its incommunicability—and so effacing a vital, ineffable otherness proffered by the other idiom.

Even so, things are more complicated. For translation is very much at work within Derrida's "French" texts; the question, the problem or the concept but also the act of translation with its textual effects and defects. For instance, at a certain point (p. 75), Derrida discusses a passage in Yerushalmi where the expression "dramatic evidence" figures in the English original. In his French text (p. 120), Derrida uses the translation *"évidence dramatique"* in quotation marks. Though *evidence* and *évidence* are cognates, the translation is problematic because the French word signifies primarily "something obvious," such that the French phrase alone would tend to translate more like "dramatic obviousness" than "dramatic evidence." So in the French, Derrida follows this translation with the English in parentheses, and then a chain of alternate translations or translation modifiers: proof, mark, clue, testimony . . . archive. These words serve to correct the translation, reorienting the sense of *évidence* to better approximate the meaning of *evidence,* so many linguistic exhibits displayed to incriminate the felicity of such a unitary accounting for this uncountable noun.

How to translate this sequence from *Mal d'archive* into English? The correct solution would no doubt have been to restore in a word the "dramatic evidence" of Yerushalmi's text, rendering five lines of French in two English words. And yet this approach too would have been guilty of economic infidelity, because in the momentum of its verbose rendition, the French translation is not simply a translation. It displaces, replaces as a translation must, and in the commotion it says more, it does more, it goes further *in* translation, while at no point ceasing to translate. And of course a translation is a going-further, going beyond the idiomatic limitations that are the very condition of linguistic expression, of signification, of anything called culture; strictly speaking it is quite impossible since it must at once follow behind and forge ahead. So I brought "dramatic evidence" out of the parentheses, dropped *"évidence dramatique,"* and put a translation of the sequence modifying, challenging, reinforcing the translation of evidence as *évidence* in parentheses. While this has the advantage of maintaining the multiplicity and some of the hermeneutic effect of Derrida's translation in *pentimento,* it falsifies the role and motivation thus also the meaning of what is here a parenthetical correction or suggestion, but which is devoid of any reference to translation and to the fertile discrepancy between *evidence* and *évidence:* it is out of place at the very least, if inoffensive, evidently misconstrued.

The obvious counterexample arises in the several places where French phrases have been kept in French in this English translation. Where they have been translated into English *as* French or *in* French in English. Untranslated in the translation, translated as untranslatable yet translated all the same. Page 78: "*L'Un se fait violence.* The One makes itself violence." In a strange though entirely workaday heterolingual *mise en abyme,* these two sentences translate the first one of themselves. They may not succeed very well, but neither one, alone, would have sufficed. In fact, the second sentence, which is a sort of word-for-word transposition of the first, serves rather as an aid for reading the French in light of what follows. Because the true translation of this sentence already followed it in the French edition: "It violates and does violence to itself but it also institutes itself as violence . . ." as I have translated it here. One might prefer to call it an intralingual explication, which would not be false, but this is also a translation, crossing the internal boundaries of the language, letting its foreignnesses make themselves at home, the text opening to its "domestic outside" (p. 19), as Derrida says in reference to the "psyche." So even the documented originality of an archive cannot cleanse it of such corruption; an archive may always be in the process of translating to itself and from itself, by itself.

Hence one reason why "the archive always holds a problem for translation," why it is "at once offered and unavailable for translation" (p. 90). However, there is another brand of translation, one that is more originary, some would say more metaphorical,[2] and which bears in it the very possibility of any hope for the transfigurative folly that goes by this name. An edifying artifice, the remains

2. But a metaphor is also a translation. Only the question of economy carries a different weight. The one's loss may well be the other's gain.

of a singular event—which should naturally leave nothing of itself behind—an archive is there for those who cannot communicate with such a solipsistic solitude in the presence and the present of its untimely happening. For while an archive may not be an end, it is only a beginning. It is not *the* beginning, and it never contains its own beginning. It can only be a translation of its conception. This is what is recounted by the *Preamble,* what is put into practice there. The archive of such an inimitable occurrence, its place of consignation in the form of a brief interlude between *Exergue* and *Foreword,* the *Preamble* is in fact the lengthy inscription of the retrospective contents of "an instant of no duration" (p. 26). Its pages unfold a unitary and timeless event with an "explication" in three wordy "meanings." On the telephone, during a conversation (but was it in French or in English?) about the title of a lecture that was yet to be written, the word *impression* imposed itself as by its own volition, automatically.

This is indeed the paradigm of translation's universal shortcomings, that is, its spatial and temporal thriftlessness, its literal disproportion. Because, while there may be correlation between an event and its textual relation, there is unfailingly strict incommensuration. Translation always operates at an economic loss.[3] In other words, the only thing that is properly untranslatable is idiomatic economy itself.

Yet Derrida also warns against holding the "technical prosthesis to be a secondary and accessory exteriority" (p. 92), against blind confidence in the possibility of a simple archaeology of the archive, through which the archive might disappear into thin air "so as to let the *origin* present itself in person. Live, without mediation and without delay. Without even the memory of a translation, once the intense work of translation has succeeded" (p. 93).[4] Because when the stones begin talking to set things straight in Freud's excava-

3. See note 15, pp. 78–79. Here too, an extemporaneous if not instantaneous "response" is clarified in three discrete remarks.

4. It seems impertinent to ask whether this "memory" which we may thus expect to be implicated in anything like an encounter with anything like an origin comes under *mnēmē,* under *anamnēsis* or under *hypomnēma:* this must be a memory from before the division into different types of memories, an impure memory of the impurity of an origin.

tional reverie, it is as if the archaeologist had succeeded in putting the archivist out of work. And the translator too, of course. Yet these stones are archives, and everyone knows that archives do not speak. Not even answering machines. Only the living answer. And what is more, in Freud's scenario, these archives turn out to be bilingual, they are themselves already translations of themselves, they speak a dead language and a living one, Greek and German for example, a bit like Hanold in his encounter with Gradiva, or at least a dead-and-forgotten dead language and a less dead one which will permit them in turn to be "deciphered and translated" (p. 93). So these stones, archives yielding "undreamed-of information about the events of the remote past," can hardly be taken for pure *archē*: if the archaeological discoveries are "self-explanatory," it is only insofar as they already reflect a prodigious amount of archival toil, and not at all because the events they record could "talk" without archivization. It is certainly not without significance that they should be hybrid, dead/living, ghostly. That stones, which ought to be dead, should talk, which only the living ought to do; nor that this event should be reenacted, performed in a particular way here, where the "*Stones talk!*" in italics, with an exclamation point, and above all in Latin, the dead language living in Freud's own hybrid text.

For if *Archive Fever* can be written down to an instant, it is the instant or the instantaneous event as overdetermination. In other words, "impure," exceeding itself, uncontained, calling for its archivization because already containing the seeds of its own archive. Divided in, and of itself. Calling but not necessarily answering for its archive. Because one can scarcely believe that when called upon as if to bear witness to its singularity or its originality, to the original singularity that it is, an event any more than a living being "ever responds in an absolutely living and infinitely well-adjusted manner, without the least automatism, without ever having an archival technique overflow the singularity of an event . . ." (p. 62). Without some answering machine effect, some spectrality in the response and thus dead in the living. Which is to say that the *impression,* the unique moment of archivization, "produces as much as it records the event" (p. 17), while nonetheless being the condition of its potential repetition; it never neutrally consigns a preexistent archivable content in a simple manner. Conversely, insofar as it is archivable, an event is always *archiving:* an event is an archiving act even if there may not be a "proper" archive and even if the archive of an event, as its interpretation, must always remain open. And this is where the question of archival technology is so significant, for it "conditions . . . the *impression,* before the division between printed and printer" (p. 18). What is the printed here? Is it the archive, or the printed content, i.e. what is archived? And is the printer the event that leaves its imprint, that is archived, or the "structure that prints"? Yes, beforehand we do not know.

There is the foot and there is the ash. But as Gradiva's sole, or Hanold's for that matter, or so many others', touches the ground, the foot, the leg, the ash and the earth below serve together as a sort of machine, a momentary printing press that will leave the archive even as it disappears forever. And this is the truth of the event of course, the true event of the event, neither material nor historical: "before the division," as the living and the dead may mingle their steps, and we'll never know for sure who's who or what's what.

Right on the ash, Derrida says, even if it makes no sense. And: *la cendre même.*

Works Cited

Benjamin, Walter. *Über den Begriff der Geschichte [Theses on the Philosophy of History]. Gesammelte Schriften.* Vol. 1. Ed. Rolf Tiedemann. Frankfurt am Main: Suhrkamp, 1980.

Brenner, Frederic, and Yosef Hayim Yerushalmi. *Marranes.* Paris: Difference, 1992.

Combe, Sonia. *Archives interdites: Les peurs françaises face à l'histoire contemporaine.* Paris: Albin Michel, 1994.

Derrida, Jacques. *D'un ton apocalyptique adopté naguère en philosophie.* Paris: Galilée, 1983.

————. *Force de loi: Le "fondement mystique de l'autorité."* Paris: Galilée, 1994.

————. *Politiques de l'amitié.* Paris: Galilée, 1994.

————. "Préjugés: Devant la loi." *La faculté de juger.* Paris: Minuit, 1985.

————. *Specters of Marx.* Trans. Peggy Kamuf. New York: Routledge, 1994. Trans. of *Spectres de Marx.* Paris: Galilée, 1994.

————. *Writing and Difference.* Trans. Alan Bass. Chicago: U of Chicago P, 1978. Trans. of *L'écriture et la différence.* Paris: Seuil, 1967.

Freud, Sigmund. *The Complete Letters of Sigmund Freud to Wilhelm Fliess, 1887–1904.* Trans. and ed. Jeffrey Moussaieff Masson. Cambridge, MA: Harvard UP, 1985.

————. *The Standard Edition of the Complete Psychological Works of Sigmund Freud.* Trans. James Strachey. London: Hogarth, 1953–74. [*SE*]

Yerushalmi, Yosef Hayim. *Freud's Moses: Judaism Terminable and Interminable.* New Haven: Yale UP, 1991.

————. *Zakhor: Jewish History and Jewish Memory.* 1982. New York: Schocken, 1989.